BITCOIN:

Beyond the Hype and Speculation

DAVID W HUFFMAN SR.

BITCOIN:

Beyond the Hype and Speculation

TABLE OF CONTENTS

INTRODUCTION

Why Bitcoin? Good question. It's a question I've been asked many times since I began accumulating and mining Bitcoin in 2020. My first exposure to Bitcoin was in 2013, but I dismissed it because most of the people raving about it were what I call hipster doofuses. It's a term I use to describe individuals who seem to know everything but have never worked a day in their lives. You know the type: they think they've found the shortcut to success and wealth because they're smarter than you. Always a new get-rich-quick scheme. They laugh at you working like a dog to provide for your family while they breeze through life enjoying themselves at the expense of someone else, usually a parent who can't say no. Perhaps that's a little harsh, but had I heard about Bitcoin from someone who woke up and went to work each day, I might have embraced it much sooner.

Covid changed a lot of things, and it certainly changed me. Suffering with my first Covid diagnosis in March 2020, I sat in a chair for seventeen days consciously struggling to breathe in and out. A difficult time for sure, but it forced me to sit idly. I don't recommend getting Covid so you can slow down and do nothing for a while, but those seventeen days allowed me to do nothing but think. And think I did. What was it all for? Why did I work so hard for so long to have it all end like this? The world was shutting down, and our small business, a little distillery at Lake of the Ozarks, Missouri, was no longer producing revenue to provide for our family or the families of our employees.

Yes, we had cash reserves to survive for a period of time, but once the government began printing large amounts of money, the value of those cash reserves diminished rapidly. We all understand inflation, but at a deeper level, inflation is really theft—theft of the value you have worked so hard to obtain, theft of the financial security we all strive for and spend a good portion of our lives in pursuit of.

This is where Bitcoin came into the picture. As I began to search for ways to preserve the value accumulated over a lifetime of work, I began to see with more clarity just what Bitcoin could be. Maybe it's money, and there are those who argue that position. But I tend to see it as a store of value, a safe place to preserve the wealth created from your efforts. It's much like purchasing gold or real estate and holding them—a store of value with a limited supply that can't be diluted by creating more. There are twenty-one million Bitcoin; that's it, no more.

This book is intended to introduce you to the idea of Bitcoin. I regularly visit with many people I grew up with in rural southeastern Iowa, and when asked about the building at the edge of our distillery parking lot making all the noise, I tell them it's a Bitcoin mining shed. They look at me with amusement and curiosity. I don't go into a lecture about the merits of Bitcoin, but I do offer a short explanation, which is usually met with an eye roll. Someone famous once said that you don't condemn the ignorant; you educate them. So this book is my attempt to open the minds of those who have no idea about Bitcoin. It's not intended to be exhaustive, as I certainly am not a writer, nor do I have the intellect to get too deep into the topic.

But I do offer the following pages as an introduction to a very complex topic and hope you will read with an open mind and follow this beginning effort to a more detailed pursuit of knowledge about Bitcoin.

Chapter 1

Introduction to Money and Its Evolution

Money . . . Whether you claim to love it or hate it, one thing is true about all of us: we all could use more of it. Most people will spend the majority of their lives working for it. Money is the measuring stick of value you have brought to the world. It is generally true that people who have more money probably have created more value for others. Not always, of course; there are always exceptions to every rule, such as winning the lottery or inheriting wealth, but for the most part, if you have done something people value, they will pay you for it.

To be considered "rich" in the United States, you need to be able to put your hands on at least $2 million (Kilroy, 2023), but the median household income is only about $70,000 (Semega & Kollar, 2022). Did you know the average person will spend a quarter of their life working just to pay his/her tax obligations (Wheelwright, 2018, pg. 3), or as we have seen since Covid, inflation could eat into your savings by as much as 17 percent in a single year (Kerr, 2022)?

Learning the secrets of financial breakthrough is vital if you want the freedom necessary to enjoy your life's fullest potential and explore this vast, beautiful world we live in. One possible way you can achieve this is with Bitcoin.

Why We Need Money

Money is the score, the ledger with which we keep track of the exchange of goods and services between people. It makes the exchange much simpler by using money as the accounting. It's not very practical if I have goats and you have fruits and vegetables and we don't both want what the other has to offer. If I need vegetables but you don't need a goat, how do we do business? Money was created so that there could be liquidity in the market. I can use money to obtain vegetables, and you can use that same money to purchase whatever you need. We no longer need to barter, because we have something we all agree has value and can be exchanged for the things we need or want. We call it money.

When governments do things that reduce the value of agreed-upon money, therein lies the problem. When our efforts to produce value are compensated with money that has less and less value, we lose the incentive to produce. Money must maintain a stable value; otherwise, we lose trust. Massive printing of new money in the US has devalued our currency and continues to devalue our currency. A dollar you earned last year will buy you much less than a dollar's worth of goods or services today. How much less is debatable. The government has a calculated inflation rate, but it's a manipulated number created out of a basket of goods and services much different than the basket of goods and services used fifty years ago or even fifteen years ago.

The point is, the number is a manufactured number and is not a true reflection of the actual inflation rate. We must work harder and more hours today for the same value that took less effort and time just one year ago. Inflation will eventually take all of your value.

The Secret to Success

Putting more sweat into the game is not likely to get you out of the nine-to-five grind. In the words of Shaan Puri: "If hard work equals success, then why isn't my janitor driving a Bentley?" (Puri, 2023, 05:19). He goes on to explain our chances of getting ahead financially are determined rather by the *type* of work we do, *how* we go about doing it, and the business *relationships* we form around it. Bitcoin will help transform your life in these key areas.

Imagine for a moment that ancient civilizations competed using their own cultures' technologies. Would the civilizations that discovered the wheel be working harder than the ones that did not? Of course they would be.

But would how *hard* a person worked in such a competition matter more than the *tools* he had access to? Would the amount of sweat expended determine who reaped the greatest rewards, or would the cleverness of the strategy employed be more expedient?

In this way, Bitcoin is a lot like the invention of the wheel in regard to money. It isn't just a new currency, but a new *type* of currency. This brand-new idea is changing the way we think about our relationship with money and the powers controlling it.

But before we learn how to use Bitcoin to buy our freedom and the life of our dreams, it's important to review the flawed currencies responsible for our current financial predicament. Bitcoin was created as a response to their failures.

A Brief History of Money

Bitcoin is the most high-tech form of currency in existence. Before it, however, lies a long trail of the fossils of our finance past.

Why are those currencies no longer in use? What led to their demise? And how did their collapse affect the lives of those who traded their precious time for them?

In the remote past, cowrie and wampum shells were used as currency, along with whale teeth and disks of limestone, until metal coins were first used in the seventh century BC. Paper money is believed to have been first issued by the Chinese around 1000 AD, and since then we have seen the rise and fall of the gold standard and the creation of the first credit cards during the 1950s (Tikkanen & Vaughan, 2020). But no one is satisfied with money itself. What we truly desire is purchasing *power*.

Purchasing power is not guaranteed, however. Imagine if you had traded the majority of your years in this world (years you could have spent with your loved ones), wearying your body with physical labor to secure German *papiermarks*, which by November 1923 had a yearly inflation rate of 325 million percent; or Austrian *pengő*, whose largest printed denomination was 100 quintillion (100,000,000,000,000,000,000) (Dehner, 2009). You don't want to exchange your limited time in this world for something with such plummeting value, do you?

The Need for Financial Independence

The United States dollar was once backed with gold, but since that policy was discontinued, inflation has wreaked havoc on people's savings. Half of your working years could be spent paying for the government's printing of new money (Mubaslat, 2020, 03:12).

When the government reaches its debt limit, the solution is always to print more money. With more dollars available, the cost of everything rises, creating inflation. This is a stealth tax on the poor, since they are the ones who suffer the most from inflation. And the majority of the money printed (or simply typed into existence as numbers on a screen) is mostly given to large corporations and special interest groups.

As Daron Acemoglu and James Robinson state in their book *Why Nations Fail,* "There is no necessity for a society to develop or adopt the institutions best for economic growth or the welfare of its citizens, because other institutions may be even better for those who control politics and political institutions" (Acemoglu et al., 2013, pg. 44). In the years following the creation of the Federal Reserve, the United States dollar has lost over nine-tenths of its value (Paul, 2019). The value of Bitcoin, conversely, has risen from US$0.39 in 2010 to its current value of nearly US$30,000 (Wallabit Media, 2017).

Federal Reserve historian G. Edward Griffin read the letters and transcribed debates of the men who were responsible for writing and passing the legislation creating this infamous institution.

In his research, he discovered it was the mission of these men to convince Congress to transfer to them *exclusive* authority under the Constitution to coin the nation's money (Corbett, 2014).

As Article I, Section 8, Clause 5 of the Constitution states: "[The Congress shall have Power . . .] To coin Money, regulate the Value thereof, and of foreign Coin, and fix the Standard of Weights and Measures" (Cornell Law School, 2021). Unfortunately for the fate of the US dollar, these banking elites succeeded in convincing the representatives of "We the People" to relinquish their constitutional power over the nation's money supply, and their civic duty to "promote the general welfare, and secure the blessings of liberty," as stated in the preamble to the Constitution.

President Franklin D. Roosevelt warned us financial powers trump governmental powers and have done so "since the days of Andrew Jackson" (Roosevelt, 1950, pg. 373). Indeed, the only time the United States had no national debt was when president Andrew Jackson put an end to its previous central bank. Roosevelt reckoned the citizens of the nation would have to fight against the new central bank, the Federal Reserve, in a battle destined to be even more grandiose.

This begs the question: what are banks anyway, and why do we need them? Could there be a better system? Will modern man ever sever his dependency upon financial institutions? How does Bitcoin offer us an opportunity to break the shackles which have held man and his wealth captive for millennia?

What Makes a Currency Secure?

None of us want to see the value of our hard-earned savings decrease, but it is a sobering reality we all must confront, though many would rather not think about it. What factors cause one currency to succeed where others fail? And why is Bitcoin the ideal solution to these problems?

In his TEDx Talk, "What is Money? And Could Bitcoin Be the Best One?", Jad Mubaslat lays out four properties of an optimum currency: *durability, divisibility, ease of transfer,* and *guaranteed scarcity* (Mubaslat, 2020). While gold does have inherent value, as it is durable and rare, it is not widely used as currency due to it being lacking in the other two qualities: namely it is cumbersome to transport and practically impossible for the average consumer to divide into smaller units.

In this book, we will explain how Bitcoin perfectly encapsulates all four qualities of an ideal currency. We know money must be durable, and Bitcoin is certainly durable, as it exists on the strongest, most secure decentralized computer network ever created in the history of the world. It's divisible into what are known as "Satoshis"; 100 million Satoshis equal one Bitcoin. It has an outstanding ease of transfer. You can send Bitcoin all over the world in a matter of seconds electronically. And it has guaranteed scarcity. There will only ever be 21 million Bitcoin. No more.

The Great Recession

Rising out of the 2007–2009 financial crisis, Bitcoin entered the equation. "As millions of people lost their homes, jobs, and savings"

(Duignan, 2023) and the poverty rate sharply increased, the average person's awareness of the flaws inherent in the current financial system grew as the topic became discussed more openly on television and radio.

Dubbed "The Great Recession," this disaster had many new books written about it, and virtually everyone had a neighbor or friend whose life was deeply affected by it. Documentarians muse about how our daily lives are still shaped by this period in ways many of us do not realize (Altraide, 2022, 21:33).

On the heels of this tragedy, an anonymous computer programmer imparted a gift to the world in the form of a novel currency with technological innovation at its core, engineered around the flaws of its predecessors. Since the blame for the crisis was unanimously pegged on the policies of third parties (i.e., financial institutions), this mysterious person or group devised a way to free consumers from dependency on them.

His name (be it his birth name or a programmer alias) is Satoshi Nakamoto. In the first transaction to ever use this new currency, he forever enshrined the spirit of Bitcoin in the form of a *Times* newspaper headline from January 3, 2009: "Chancellor on brink of second bailout for banks" (Williams, 2021). He, like many others around the globe, was done playing by the rigged rules of the financial elite.

Why Bitcoin Changed Everything

As Satoshi plainly stated in a February 2009 promotion of his new invention, "The root problem with conventional currency is all the trust that's required to make it work. The central bank must be trusted not to debase the currency, but the history of fiat currencies is full of breaches of that trust" (Nakamoto, 2009).

Similarly to how the dawn of peer-to-peer file sharing ushered in a new era for the music industry (one in which the poor gained more power while the wealthy were forced to cede some), Satoshi's foundational white paper, entitled "Bitcoin: A Peer-to-Peer Electronic Cash System," laid out the blueprint for creating a currency that does not require a trusted third party in order to be stored, transferred, earned, or spent.

How this innovation benefits you is the bank, which foreclosed on your neighbor's home or lost your savings while attempting to flip it for profit, could potentially be rendered obsolete. This is not merely a once-in-a-century opportunity, but a once-in-a-millennium opportunity at least! And what's more amazing is the creator of this technology opted to never patent it or even trademark the name. The original white paper can be found at the end of this book.

Chapter 2

The Birth of Bitcoin

Who Is Satoshi Nakamoto?

In 2021, while the economies of nations around the world were still suffering due to the COVID-19 pandemic, the price of Bitcoin surged to its all-time high at over $68,000 (Coinbase, 2023), smashing the previous year's milestone of $19,000 (La Monica, 2020). Because of this unprecedented sticker shock, Bitcoin was beginning to win a place in the hearts and minds of those who had previously been its skeptics.

Even longtime critics like talk show host Alex Jones were finally warming up to the cryptocurrency. To celebrate Bitcoin's historic achievement, Alex called Bitcoin advocate Max Kieser back on his show in order to offer him an apology for not accepting his gift of 10,000 free Bitcoin, which Max had offered to him when they were worth around a dollar each. During this interview, Max declared Bitcoin to be one of mankind's most important revolutions:

> [Bitcoin separates] the State from money. We saw something like that in the middle ages with the separation of Church and State when the Gutenberg press came around and it put knowledge into everybody's hands. And we had an enormous separation in the beginning of the Renaissance. Now we've got a separation of State and money with this technology called Bitcoin, and it's totally upending the apple cart. It is changing everything around the world. It's changing what the definition of money is, and people are freaking out, understandably (Jones, 2021, 04:13).

The hype surrounding Bitcoin became a pop culture sensation that year, as its reputation began to rival gold among investors. Indeed, as the BBC reported, Bitcoin had managed to surpass the price of gold four years earlier (BBC, 2017).

At the height of this new-found infatuation with Bitcoin, a bust was erected in a public square in Budapest, the capital city of Hungary, serving as a memorial to Bitcoin's inventor (Spike, 2021). This vague bronze casting of Satoshi's unknown visage lauds him as not merely a figure in pop culture, not merely a skilled programmer, but more akin to a religious leader.

But who is he? What does he look like? And why can no one find him now?

Those who financed the creation of his statue in Budapest invited him to its unveiling, in hopes he would come forward and his true identity would finally be revealed to the world. Despite the notoriety and prestige destined to be showered upon him at the event, he nevertheless chose to remain hidden in the shadows.

Ten years earlier, on April 23, 2011, he had announced he was quitting Bitcoin. His resignation was delivered publicly to the world. It read simply, "I've moved on to other things. It's in good hands" (Thompson, 2023).

Among those who worked with Satoshi during the years in which he was actively involved with the project's development, none of them ever had the privilege of meeting the man in person (CNBC, 2017, 01:13). So far as we know, not one Bitcoin programmer knows what Satoshi looks like.

What could be Mr. Nakamoto's motive for hiding? Did he fear the wrath of the world's financial titans? Did he foresee government persecution? How much Bitcoin did he accumulate before taking a bow?

Bitcoin investor Ben Yu suggested in an interview with CNBC that if Satoshi were to resurface now, he could become a "spiritual leader" (CNBC, 2017, 05:20). With mainstream news publishing articles warning of a Bitcoin "civil war" (Kelion, 2017), strong leadership is needed to keep the Bitcoin community from splitting up. Who could be more fit to lead than the man who gave birth to this revolution?

Searching for the Real Satoshi

Attempts to locate Satoshi once resulted in a Japanese-American man's life being uprooted in a media cyclone. Dorian Satoshi Nakamoto was outed by *Newsweek* writer Leah Goodman as the real thing. *This* Nakamoto, however, claimed not to be *the* Nakamoto.

Dorian called the police as soon as the reporter confronted him at his home (Goodman, 2014). After spending a week and a half with the gaze of the world directed at his home and his family, he issued this response to Goodman's article:

I did not create, invent, or otherwise work on Bitcoin. I unconditionally deny the *Newsweek* report . . . I have not been able to find steady work as an engineer or programmer for ten years. I have worked as a laborer, polltaker, and substitute teacher. I discontinued my internet service in 2013 due to severe financial distress. I am trying to recover from prostate surgery in October 2012 and a stroke I suffered in October of 2013. My prospects for gainful employment have been harmed because of *Newsweek*'s article. *Newsweek*'s false report has been the source of a great deal of confusion and stress for myself, my ninety-three-year-old mother, my siblings, and their families. . . . This will be our last public statement on this matter. I ask that you now respect our privacy (Goodman, 2014).

With that thread closed, it seemed the world was out of leads as to the true identity of Bitcoin's founder. But in the midst of this media blitzkrieg, the real Nakamoto broke his radio silence of three years. His one-line return to public life read as follows: "I am not Dorian Nakamoto" (Thompson, 2023). And with that said, no one ever heard from him again.

Regardless of the efforts the real Satoshi put into divorcing himself from the project—even going as far as to remove his name from the software before vanishing (Rizzo, 2021)—his name will always be tied to it. For what a cent is to a dollar, a Satoshi is to a Bitcoin. The smallest division of a single Bitcoin is called a "Satoshi." This fact alone makes it unlikely advocates of the cryptocurrency will forget the man who once was the faceless face of digital coinage.

Like a canceled sequel to a beloved film or the breakup of your favorite band after they just released their best album, his abrupt departure will always perplex the community. For this one man set in motion a revolution that could very well crush the big banking cartels, which even governments have historically feared. Suddenly and without warning, Satoshi's presence in our lives dissipated into the fog of speculative headlines.

What Caused Satoshi to Disappear?

The last documented private correspondence from him was an email he sent to Bitcoin's number two man at the time, Gavin Andresen, in which Satoshi asked Gavin to stop casting the project in a conspiracy theory type of light to the press by referring to him as a "mysterious shadowy figure" (Blockchain Media Group, 2019).

Mr. Andresen responded to let Satoshi know he had been invited to speak at an event put on by the United States Central Intelligence Agency: more specifically, an annual conference hosted by In-Q-Tel on emerging technologies and how they could prove beneficial to the operations of the CIA (OnlyOneTV, 2011). Satoshi ignored the invitation and ceased all communications with Andresen (Nakamoto Studies Institute, 2011).

Fear of government retaliation would not have been unreasonable and may have been a factor in his sudden exodus. In the words of Jameson Lopp, chief technology officer of Casa (a company that provides Bitcoin secure storage): "The smartest thing Satoshi did after creating Bitcoin was to disappear" (Blockchain Media Group, 2019).

Another possible reason he vanished was the burgeoning criticism and distrust aimed at him, which had been mounting in internet forums during the time before his departure from the project. In these forums, Satoshi was once lauded as a mastermind. But as the project evolved out of a pipedream of a small band of hobbyist programmers into a worldwide paradigm shift, these sites quickly morphed into echo chambers where crowds of newcomers vented their frustrations with and paranoia of Bitcoin's creator, spouting unfounded conspiracy theories about who he was and what his intentions were:

> As criticisms escalated, Satoshi appears to have remained active and online, but even he would struggle to keep pace with the volume and urgency of conversation ahead. By November, everywhere it seemed, users were out to test the boundaries Satoshi had set, some claiming his design was flawed, while others went so far as to argue his system did little more than unjustly enrich himself (Rizzo, 2021).

A few months before the CIA conference, in October of 2010, one user in the developer log likened Satoshi's power to choose the number of Bitcoins that should exist to God's power to choose how much gold or silver should exist (thrashaholic, 2010). The following month, another user in the same log called him a money launderer (mpkomara, 2010), and the month after that, he was called a "dictator" by a forum user claiming the "right to reject/fork his project" (kiba, 09).

That same Winter, Gavin Andresen was asked what would happen if Satoshi went "rogue"; to which Gavin responded, "If Satoshi goes rogue, then the project forks" (Andresen, 2010). This message paints a bleak picture of just how alone and distrusted Satoshi must have felt, as he no doubt lurked in these forums and might have seen even his number two man posting about how eager he was to fork the code and continue without him.

Another programmer chimed in: "If one day Satoshi says, 'Okay, guys, it was just a joke with this Bitcoin thing. I'm closing down the project,' then we (the hackers) would simply fork the code, move to another forum, and pick up where we left here" (ShadowOfHarbringer, 2010). And another: "The minute Satoshi does something crazy and not supported by the community is the moment the protocol/codebase is truly forked" (jgarzik, 2010).

A *fork*, in programming terminology, is when a codeset (typically of an open-source nature, such as Bitcoin) is copied and then developed into two different builds by separate programmers who hold irreconcilable visions for the future of the code.

The launchpad of the Bitcoin project was the Bitcoin white paper, which was released freely to the public by Mr. Nakamoto on Halloween day, 2008. Let's peek inside this humble essay that set the world on fire and forced its author into hiding.

How Satoshi's White Paper Started a Revolution

If there is one thing people with power hate, it's seeing another power rise up to challenge their own. Just ask American oil industry titan John D. Rockefeller, who is famously quoted as saying, "Competition is a sin" (Harvey, 2017).

Just as wealth begets wealth, power accumulates more power. This is true because once authority metastasizes into authoritarianism, the powerful award themselves the privilege of deciding how much power they should have. This can happen in government, academia, and even organized religion.

While most people spend October 31 each year thinking about refined sugar and things that go bump in the night, historians remember it as the day Martin Luther nailed his ninety-five criticisms of the papacy to the door of Germany's Castle Church: an act of defiance that jump-started the Protestant Reformation. Four hundred and ninety-one years later *to the day*, Satoshi shared the Bitcoin white paper with the world, which, not unlike Luther's complaints with the religious establishment of his day, repudiated the financial sector: specifically, its corruption and its unwillingness to hold itself accountable.

Luther enlightened Christians as to how they could still adhere to the teachings of their founders while cutting ties with the hierarchy that had sprung up in their name ("the separation of Church and State"). Similarly, Satoshi's paper proved how the separation of *money* and State could manifest in a secure, private, and legal manner.

And the religious connotations don't stop there. Satoshi spent three years guiding his flock before leaving his work in their hands: the same amount of time Jesus spent in his earthly ministry before exiting public life and leaving his commission in the hands of his disciples. And then there's the "genesis" block, which shares its name with the foundational book of the Bible. This first of blocks on the chain took six days to mine (Blockchain Media Group, 2019), just as God spent six days creating the heaven, earth, and sea, resting on the seventh day, according to the book of Genesis.

The first fifty Bitcoins ever were awarded in the verification of that block and have to this day *never* been spent. If you have the wallet address, you can check it out for yourself ("1A1zP"). Last time I checked, it had 72 BTC in it, since people have been sending small amounts of Bitcoin to the address as if it were a sanctimonious offering (Blockchair, 2023).

This initial block is hardcoded so as to give the blockchain a starting point and an anchor (Redman, 2023), meaning the money in it cannot be spent (or so we are told). It's quite an homage to Bitcoin's founder (as it is commonly believed he is in control of the wallet). Its existence is a necessity, but it functions, perhaps unintentionally, as a shrine to the dawning of the cryptocurrency revolution.

But what is a block anyway? Well, since Satoshi's ideas were "released under an MIT public license in 2008 for all to learn from, share, and enjoy" (Leech, 2022), we are free to analyze every aspect of his invention in great detail. This is in direct contrast to the often-secretive operations of traditional financial institutions.

What Is Blockchain?

A *block* in the context of Bitcoin is a cluster of data, including transactions. A *blockchain* is like a timeline created with data, similar to a train with its linked set of cars, each one carrying its own goods (Feign, 2022). While banking institutions, even going back far in the past, had *ledgers* (records of transactions and holdings), those were nothing more than insecure pieces of paper that were kept secret from the public eye.

This type of system requires tremendous trust in the institution holding the ledger. Bitcoin, however, annihilates the need for any type of trust in a third party, because every person using the network has a copy of the ledger (Joint Economic Committee, 2018, pg. 205). It's easy to identify a ledger that contains fraud when there are so many matching copies.

This is one of several ways Bitcoin makes performing fraudulent activity more cumbersome than honest activity, thereby making it impractical to attempt on the network.

If you know a certain Bitcoin wallet address, you will be able to see the transactions made with said wallet, but not the name of the person making the transactions (Urban Caffeine, 2021). This type of system relies on verification over trust.

Back before the proliferation of credit cards and the advent of internet shopping, most people carried cash with them, so there was no need for a third party (i.e., a bank) to carry out a transaction between a business and its customer. But since the government stopped printing higher denominations of currency, and since nearly every business began accepting debit and credit cards, those days are long gone.

The genius of Bitcoin is bringing us back to the simplicity and control of the days when cash was king. What's even more amazing is that it is doing it in a way that accommodates the new normal of doing business online.

How Does Bitcoin Keep Data Secure?

Satoshi was not an island. The technological blueprint laid out in his white paper references the previous work of one Adam Back: a project called Hashcash, which dates back to the 1990s. Satoshi's work borrowed heavily from Back's: specifically, Hashcash's "proof-of-work" function, which makes up the core of Bitcoin mining (Bitcoin.it, 2022).

Cryptography is the study and practice of protecting information from unauthorized access. It comes from two Greek words meaning "secret writing." Examples of its use can be found in ancient history among Egyptian hieroglyphics and third-century Sanskrit. There was also the "Caesar cipher," which was used by Julius Caesar himself in the first century BC (Web3 Working Group, 2022, 01:28) to deliver encoded messages to his generals.

Encryption refers to the actual process of encoding data in order to protect it from being read by unauthorized individuals. Encryption can be either *symmetric* or *asymmetric*. Symmetric encryptions uses a single key to both encrypt and decrypt data. Asymmetric encryption employs a dual-key design: one to encrypt data and another to decrypt it (Web3 Working Group, 2022, 05:19).

Since asymmetric encryption is much slower than symmetric, a hybrid combination was formulated and named Transport Layer Security (TLS). This became the most common form of encryption in use on the internet, due to its balance between speed and security (Web3 Working Group, 2022, 09:25).

Bitcoin utilizes the cryptographic hash algorithm SHA-256 (256-bit Secure Hash Algorithm) in mining (the process of introducing new coins to the network) and in the creation of Bitcoin addresses (Mycryptopedia, 2022). Satoshi mentioned it specifically on page 3 of his white paper, in a section entitled "Proof-of-Work."

SHA-256 is not, technically speaking, encryption. SHA-256 does not have a key, so it is neither symmetric nor asymmetric. A cryptographic hash function like SHA-256 takes an input of any length and maps it to an output of a specific length.

Until the age of computing came along, the words *cryptography* and *encryption* were used interchangeably. But in modern times, the word *encryption* came into a specific use regarding electronic computational processes of encoding data.

We won't get too deep into the technical jargon here. What's important for you to understand is this algorithm has never been observed giving the same output for two different inputs. Every unique set of data passed through it gets turned into a completely unique "string" (a series of characters). You could call it a DNA test for your data—and it's probably more reliable than one!

To put it simply, let's say you had one of those fancy decoder rings, like in the movie *A Christmas Story*. Two *different* data inputs should not both generate the *same* output ("Drink more Ovaltine"). This aspect of SHA-256 makes it the ideal algorithm for Bitcoin to use, since it flawlessly gives every Bitcoin transaction a "serial number" if you will, which is called a *hash*.

Building on the ingenuity of this cryptographic hash algorithm, blockchains are assembled in this manner: blocks are converted into hashes (the 32-byte maps of characters generated by SHA-256), which are then time-stamped. Since each block includes the time-stamped hash of the block before it, this creates an immutable timeline of all the activities on the network. We'll get more into the specific technological processes of Bitcoin operations in a coming chapter on mining.

Think about it this way: committing fraud on a network as secure as blockchain would be similar to lying in court about your interaction with a police officer, when his full bodycam footage was available for all to view online. That wouldn't be very wise or practical, would it?

Now imagine you had the footage professionally altered in order to convince the jury of your fraudulent account of the police interaction. Unfortunately for you, however, countless copies of the genuine original footage had already been downloaded from the police department's YouTube channel. That's what it would be like trying to get away with fraud on the Bitcoin network, since the ledger is distributed to all—something made possible only because of the security blockchain brings.

What Is Proof-of-Work?

Proof-of-Work is the consensus mechanism currently employed by the Bitcoin network. A *consensus mechanism* is simply a way of making sure we're all on the same page. Whether you and your men are about to charge into battle against the Spartans or are ten yards from the end zone against the New England Patriots, you'd best make sure everyone is using the same play book.

Other cryptocurrencies may employ other types of consensus mechanisms, such as *proof-of-stake*. There have been calls to convert Bitcoin to a proof-of-stake system, as a means of cutting energy expenditure. Proof-of-Work intentionally uses large amounts of computational power by pitting computers against one another in a competition to solve high-level mathematical problems. The incentive for solving these problems is the mining reward we discussed earlier (currently in 2023, 6.25 BTC).

The idea behind this is "nobody can flood the network with fake transactions due to the high cost and difficulty level. Satoshi recommends the algorithm change its difficulty based on how frequently blocks are created, in order to keep up with technological advances" (Vermaak, 2023). It's a bit like living in a high-rent gated community: you're a lot less likely to have troublemakers in a community like that, since people are spending so much to live there.

Since it requires such a tremendous investment of CPU time (necessitating costly electric bills and expensive computers), criminals are dissuaded from their attempts. And since there is an incentive to participate in the verification of blocks (the mining reward now, and after the last Bitcoin has been mined, transaction fees), it makes more sense to spend your CPU time on the common good of the network.

Should Bitcoin Change Consensus Mechanisms?

Should the Bitcoin network alter Satoshi's vision and embrace proof-of-stake? This would mean large amounts of computational power (and therefore energy) could be saved. Such a change would task those who hold the largest stakes in the network with validation.

Should we fundamentally change the method by which security is achieved on the Bitcoin network, contrary to Satoshi's design? What would make some so eager to advocate for such a change? Let's examine some data.

In May of 2022, CNBC ran the headline "China Is Second-Biggest Bitcoin Mining Hub as Miners Go Underground" (Browne, 2022).

In September of 2019, China accounted for 75 percent of all Bitcoin mining, while the United States accounted for only 4 percent. By January of 2022, China accounted for 21 percent, while the US accounted for 37 percent (Statista, 2023).

According to Our World in Data, in 2022 China generated 5,421.19 TWh of electricity by burning coal (commonly thought of as dirty energy), while in the United States the number was only 828.99 TWh from coal (Global Change Data Lab, 2023). Ars Technica wrote, "in 2021, China's pollution was larger than all other developed nations' put together" (De Chant, 2021). So the world's number one Bitcoin mining nation is using cleaner forms of energy, while the world's number two Bitcoin mining nation, though using less clean forms of energy, is in the process of banning Bitcoin mining altogether.

Elon Musk famously accepted Bitcoin as payment for Tesla automobiles, only to do an about-face shortly after, citing environmental impact. But according to Max Keiser, "There's about 160,000 terawatt hours of energy used on planet Earth a year, and right now Bitcoin uses one-tenth of 1 percent of that energy" (Jones, 2021, 04:50).

To put the environmental effects of Bitcoin "mining" in perspective, let's compare it with the actual mining of physical minerals here in the third dimension. To make batteries for a Tesla Roadster or similar vehicle, large amounts of rare earth minerals such as lithium and cobalt have to be brought to the surface from deep in the earth. This is done by drilling enormous holes in the ground in attempts to locate the necessary minerals.

Contrarily, we know where all the Bitcoins to be mined are located. These earth mines tend to be highly toxic, and worked by laborers who are often underage.

Rest assured, there is no seeing black and white when it comes to this nuanced issue. The world is certainly not going to end due to a minority of its computers using electricity in order to solve mathematical equations, but we should always make sure we are good stewards of our environment. Later on, we will discuss how you can begin making money with Bitcoin mining, how the mining process works, and ways it might be done sustainably. At this moment, let's take a closer look at Satoshi's white paper.

How the White Paper Remedied Digital Money's Biggest Problem

Arguably, the greatest merit of Satoshi's work is he devised a way to ensure the same money could not be spent in two different transactions, in what is known as *double-spending*.

While a physical object of value cannot be duplicated (such as a bar of gold, for example), a digital asset certainly could. I'm sure by now we've all copied and pasted something using a computer. So what's to stop someone from infinitely cloning their digital money without working for it?

How this had been accomplished before 2008 was that trust had to be placed in a third party, like PayPal, VISA, your local credit union, etc. What truly set Satoshi's work apart was he solved the double-spending problem while at the same time devising a way to do it without dependency upon third parties.

Think about it this way: somebody at one point invented the self-checkout, and now you can hardly find a human cashier in many places. Stores built decades ago may have twelve lanes for human cashiers, but only one or two will ever be open unless it's Black Friday.

Another group of people invented the fully automated fast food restaurant, which we are now seeing pop up in major cities. And now artificial intelligence is threatening to make fields like graphic design much more competitive for job seekers. How many positions in agriculture are now performed by giant machines?

Similarly to how the technological innovation of the vending machine made it possible to remove an unnecessary individual from a transaction, the Bitcoin network employs highly sophisticated and cleverly engineered systems that could one day put your bank out of business. It removes trust from the equation and replaces it with verification:

> Up until Satoshi's innovation, the double-spend was the Achilles' heel of digital currency transactions—it simply wasn't possible for a digital system to prove two, or more, different people didn't spend the same digital money without the use of an intermediary. . . . Solving the double-spend problem in the digital world makes near real-time commerce possible across the entire planet without regard to individual banking access, currency denominations or geographical location. . . . Solving the double-spend problem opened a massive technological frontier that allowed for experimentation and the design and deployment of *a new financial sector* (Barhydt, 2018).

So how was Satoshi able to solve the double-spend problem? It was done with the idea of a timestamp server.

This server takes the hash in a block of transactions and then broadcasts that hash to everyone in the bitcoin network. This timestamp proves the data in the hash wasn't created after the hash was shared. Each timestamp has the previous timestamp in its hash, which creates an immutable record of the order in which transactions took place. What this does is create a record of every Bitcoin transaction ever made, and everyone running a node has a copy of this record, better known as the blockchain.

CHAPTER 3

HOW BITCOIN SOLVES PROBLEMS WITH TRADITIONAL MONEY

Why Bitcoin Beats Fiat

If the financial systems and types of money we have had thus far were flawless, there should have been no opportunity to correct them. But the Great Recession of 2008 kindled a fire in the mind of Satoshi.

During a crisis in which six million people became unemployed in the United States alone, along with eight million losing their homes (Altraide, 2022, 28:40), Satoshi registered the domain bitcoin.org, where he would later post his white paper. According to Weng Chong of Business Insider, Satoshi had "the intention of bridging the global wealth gap" (Cheong, 2019).

The crux of the problem with traditional money is inflation. Bitcoin's value, conversely, has a proven track record of defying inflation. According to Mark Yusko, CEO of Morgan Creek Capital Management, Bitcoin could soar to $500,000 by the end of this decade (Competiello, 2019). Compare that with the currency of Venezuela, which saw over 90 percent inflation last decade. Bitcoin is immune to this, due to scarcity being baked into its design.

If the person who holds the most Bitcoin of all sold it all at once, the price would certainly dip, but only temporarily (CNBC, 2017, 03:41). Some analysts postulate Satoshi is in a position to do this, but why would he?

The same scenario has played out when large amounts of gold were sold in the past, yet the price of gold managed to climb back and even reach new heights. Why is that? Well, gold has inherent value, unlike fiat currency.

Even Satoshi argued "the traditional qualifications for money were written with the assumption that [since] there are so many competing objects in the world that are scarce, an object with the automatic bootstrap of intrinsic value will surely win out over those without intrinsic value" (Nakamoto, 2010). But does Bitcoin have intrinsic value?

We could argue Bitcoin carries with it definite value derived from its security, ease of use, privacy, and scarcity. In addition to these, there also exists its potential for programmability. There has been advocacy for the creation of applications on the Bitcoin network—as has been done with the world's number two cryptocurrency, Ethereum. Unlike traditional applications—that store user data in one place due to their centralized nature—decentralized applications (or "dapps") put users in control of their own data (Hertig, 2021).

Why Decentralization Matters

That green lock icon in your browser is the peace of mind encryption brings. Solving both the speed limitations of asymmetric encryption and the security concerns of symmetric encryption, the hybrid approach, TLS, or Transport Layer Security, was adopted en masse: a move allowing the internet we now know to evolve out of the "the information superhighway" of the late '80s and early '90s—

which to many was nothing more than a curious oddity and a passing fad.

Perhaps you remember BonziBuddy (a quasi-AI assistant proven to be malware), or one-frame-per-second animated GIFs of the United States flag. The simpler days of the internet are remembered fondly by many, but most people back then did not feel safe putting their credit card, bank account, or social security numbers online—and rightly so.

Before the TLS approach became the norm, viruses, malware, phishing, and data breaches were out of control. That's why the internet didn't really transform into the economic juggernaut it is now until the problem of security was first solved. The hurdle we had to clear in order to achieve widespread implementation of encryption back then was speed. TLS fixed that.

So if we have TLS now, why do we need to take it a step further with blockchain? Remember the title of Satoshi's paper: "Bitcoin: **A Peer-to-Peer** Electronic Cash System." You see, the problem still inherent with Transport Layer Security is data is *centralized*. Peer-to-Peer systems are inherently *decentralized*.

Let's say, for example, you have a favorite show on your preferred streaming platform. It's an original series, meaning you can *only* watch it online, and *only* on this one platform. There has never been and never will be a physical DVD or Blu-ray release.

Turn the clock forward ten years and imagine the Overton window has shifted. Now, something in that show does not live up to modern sensibilities.

A certain episode, or perhaps the entire series, is pulled from the site without warning. This sort of scenario plays out time and time again.

Since the data was centralized (i.e., was stored exclusively on the servers of the streaming platform), the show is potentially lost forever. But if it was ever distributed on a physical medium (like DVD), then there is almost no chance of losing all of the copies in existence—except for maybe an asteroid shattering the crust of the earth. So decentralized data is inherently more secure and is better for everyone.

The way TLS works is by using faster, less secure encryption (symmetric) on users' data while using slower, better encryption (asymmetric) on those symmetric keys (Web3 Working Group, 2022, 08:55). This gave the internet enough security to greenlight its rapid transformation of our world, especially regarding how we shop and do banking. Remember, however, this model relies heavily on *centralized* storage of data.

Perhaps society jumped the gun by putting all of our personal information online. Consider the Heartland Payment Systems credit card hack: an incident in 2009 where data thieves had unauthorized access to information from one hundred million transactions per month for a period of several months (Acohido, 2009). And then there's the Equifax cyberattack of 2017, which potentially exposed the social security numbers of half of all United States citizens (BBC, 2017). This stolen information is then sold on the dark web for use in illicit financial activities.

Most people go about their daily lives without spending a single thought on the fact their voting records and political affiliation are likely to have been accessed by intruders, along with potentially their social security number, credit card details, and perhaps even medical records. All of these tragedies occurred because of the one fundamental flaw in the way corporations implement encryption (i.e., to transfer massive amounts of data to themselves). When user and consumer data is stored in one location, it takes hackers less time to find it. Blockchain, being decentralized, provides the perfect solution to this problem.

How Decentralization Puts Power in the Hands of the People

We've all heard the old adage about not putting all of our eggs in one basket. Blockchain encodes and exchanges data at the peer-to-peer level. The key benefit of this is the data is spread out in more locations, making more computationally expensive (and therefore slower) methods of encryption feasible to implement due to smaller, more direct transfers. The Bitcoin protocol itself does not use encryption, but exchanges, websites, and wallets may (Murch, 2019) (Akashmomale, 2022).

Since asymmetric encryption requires much more computational power, big corporations often cheap out and use the inferior symmetric encryption, which is something of a placebo, since any unauthorized user who intercepts the key can read all of the data. But since a peer-to-peer system involves smaller, more local transactions, asymmetric encryption is in the cards again.

In addition to this, if hackers hypothetically manage to compromise one server, that basket (server) will not contain all the eggs (consumer data).

Decentralization not only protects users from data breaches; it also shields them from discrimination. When an industry becomes centralized, then one corporation or bureau may accumulate an unchallengeable surplus of power. When that happens, your assets can be frozen simply for falling out of favor with the central authority.

Some types of businesses are considered high-risk and can have a hard time opening an account. Not only is financial risk taken into account, but also *reputational* risk to the bank. Entrepreneurs in high-risk sectors can have their accounts shut down without warning, regardless of their many years of having an account in good standing. This sort of knee-jerk reaction from banks can kill your business overnight.

According to The Brookings Institution, access to credit, distance to the closest branch, and the costliness of account fees can vary greatly based on your zip code (Loh, 2021). Reuters cited a federal government study with data suggesting Hispanic-Americans and African-Americans were about 50 percent less likely to receive the financing they applied for, despite having an adequate credit score (Marte & Nomiyama, 2021).

Even well-known political commentators, such as Nigel Frage, or entrepreneurs who command large amounts of capital, such as Donald Trump, have had their accounts closed suddenly and without warning.

In addition to this, PayPal recently updated its Acceptable Use Policy to include a $2,500 fine for "misinformation"—though they claim to have backtracked after widespread criticism (Lima & Schaffer, 2022). Are you starting to understand why decentralization matters?

What if the loan officiator at your local bank has a particular bias against what you look like or the political pin you wore when you sat down with him? That bias can't happen with Bitcoin.

With Bitcoin, yes, all transactions are public, as well as the amount of BTC held in a particular wallet (if you happen to know the wallet address), but not the *name* of the person who holds the key to the wallet. So Bitcoin is perhaps the most *transparent* currency there is, but it is also the most private *where it counts*:

> Bitcoin is often perceived as an anonymous payment network. But in reality, Bitcoin is probably the most transparent payment network in the world. At the same time, Bitcoin can provide acceptable levels of privacy when used correctly. . . . Bitcoin addresses cannot remain fully anonymous. As the block chain is permanent . . . to protect your privacy, you should use a new Bitcoin address each time you receive a new payment (Bitcoin Project, 2013).

If your currency of choice is Bitcoin, then you can't be discriminated against by a bank teller, because there is no need for branches. Sure, someone could set up a brick-and-mortar cryptocurrency exchange if they wished to, but it's not a necessity for cryptocurrency to work.

To use Bitcoin, no one needs to see what you look like or your political affiliation, age, sex, race, or disability status.

And considering the United States saw over fifteen thousand physical bank locations close over the last decade (Loh, 2021), Bitcoin will put you ahead of the curve in terms of the direction money is going anyway (that is, *away* from the physical).

There are two billion people in the world who don't have access to traditional banking (Business Insider, 2017). Cryptocurrency can bridge a gap for anyone who has just a basic internet connection.

CHAPTER 4

THE MECHANICS OF BITCOIN TRANSACTIONS

How Easy Is It to Use Bitcoin?

Wrapping your head around Bitcoin might at first seem like a daunting task if software engineering isn't in your background. Here are some analogies to help you understand just how simple it really is.

Those of us who are past a certain age remember video rental stores. They almost always had a slot for you to drop your VHS tape in (or Betamax, if you were into the finer things). The cleverness of the design was these transactions could be conducted any time of day or night, regardless of whether the store was open or not. This system also provided *public* access to the depositing of tapes, but required *private* access for their retrieval.

While take-home rentals of video tapes may be a thing of the past, it makes a great analogy for the sending and receiving of Bitcoin. Those drop-off slots were kept in public spaces, and anyone was free to drop tapes into the slot; so, too, can anyone, if they have your wallet address, easily send you Bitcoin.

In the same way, as only the video store employee could retrieve the tapes on the other side of the wall, only the person who owns the wallet can retrieve the funds after they have been deposited (Steele, 2018).

With Bitcoin, you can generate a new wallet ID at any time. That would be like having the ability to set up new drop boxes at different locations in the city at the speed of thought. Each wallet is tied to its history of transactions, so for privacy's sake, it's not a bad idea to periodically start over.

Let's make another analogy. Think about handwritten signatures. They have long been accepted as a hallmark of identity verification, but how secure are they really? Maybe penmanship isn't one of your hobbies, but I'm sure a master of calligraphy would have no trouble counterfeiting a signature.

The signature of Donald Trump has been photographed thousands of times, and he once held what is considered to be the most powerful position in the world: the president of the United States. I'm sure there is someone out there who could have both the motivation and skill to duplicate a signature of someone who signs checks as big as he does.

Nowadays, more and more signatures are being delivered through inaccurate pin pad screens, or by a finger on smartphones. All in all, the signature is not really the gold standard it once was.

Husbands and wives have not been shy about forging each other's signatures with the other's blessing. I imagine a practice such as that could turn into something really ugly in the event of a divorce.

In terms of handwritten signatures, here in the third dimension, you're only supposed to have one. But on the Bitcoin network, all transactions have their own *unique* digital signature (99Bitcoins, 2017, 01:00). That's far more secure than a John Hancock!

Once it is signed with a totally unique signature, your transaction waits in what is called the *memory pool* until it is verified by miners. The miners group transactions into a block, and compete to have their block verified, hoping to receive a reward (99Bitcoins, 2017, 03:22).

A verified block is then added to the blockchain, where it is forever preserved in public history. Anyone can view the blockchain using a website or application known as a *block explorer*.

Never accept an unverified transaction, as it may be canceled. You will see your newly verified transaction listed with a value of 1. As new blocks are added to the chain, you will see that number increase. This timeline of verification illustrates the overwhelming security of blockchain.

Allow me to give you an example. Let's say a certain scientific hypothesis is proven as fact. Take the laws of thermodynamics, for instance. Einstein said of the second law, "It is the only physical theory of universal content, which I am convinced, within the framework of applicability of its basic concepts will never be overthrown" (Ben-Naim, 2019). Wow. Well that sounds pretty solid to me. Einstein was a pretty smart guy, so I think we should take his word on it.

Now that the science is settled on thermodynamics, we can feel secure to start basing new hypotheses on it, right? But what would happen if we jumped the gun and began proposing hypotheses upon unproven hypotheses? We might end up writing nothing more than science fiction if we did that.

Blockchain functions by the same principle. Future transactions will be stacked upon your transaction, which was verified in the past. As that happens, the verification count on the older transaction will go up and up.

Let's use another analogy. Imagine if in a murder trial, the basis of the prosecution's indictment was a supposed set of crimes committed by the defendant at a certain ski resort on a certain day. Now imagine the prosecutors did not bother to check if the defendant was actually present at said resort on the day of the crimes. Well, if the defendant can easily prove he wasn't there on that day, then the alleged *chain* of events falls apart.

In the same way, future blocks of transactions in the chain are tied to older blocks already verified. This creates multilayered security by arranging a public timeline of all events on the network literally anyone with a basic internet connection can go check for themselves using a block explorer application.

Can Bitcoin Be Hacked?

Perhaps in another biblical reference to the six-day creation from the book of Genesis, a transaction is accepted as secure once it reaches a confirmation number of 6. Since it takes about ten minutes to confirm a block, you might be waiting around an hour to see your block reach this threshold. As Coin Guides puts it:

There is no central authority to consult whether a transaction is successful or not. Since the system is decentralized, the community considers transaction confirmation numbers as a validity. There is nothing special about 6 confirmations. This number is chosen assuming that it would cost an attacker more in order to double spend. With 6 confirmations it becomes practically impossible for an attacker to re-org and reverse a transaction, [or] create an alternate chain faster than the original chain. *In Bitcoin the longest chain wins.* So [it's] not just 6 confirmations; the more on-chain confirmations your transaction has, the harder it is to rewrite (Coin Guides, 2021).

A "re-org" refers to turning back the clock: unraveling the blockchain, in a sense. This has never been done before, but was suggested as a solution to recover 7,000 BTC that were stolen when the largest cryptocurrency exchange, Binance, was hacked in 2019.

When this hack occurred, the notion of reorganizing the blockchain sparked heated debates, due to its unprecedented nature. If the plan was implemented, it would result in the creation of two different Bitcoin blockchains: *Bitcoin A* would be used by the rest of the world, and *Bitcoin B* would be used by Binance, theoretically speaking.

In a since-deleted post on social media, the head of Binance war-gamed the pros and cons of reorganizing the chain (Coin Guides, 2019). Mike Novogratz, CEO of Galaxy Investment Partners, called this "close to heresy," saying he was "shocked" the head of Binance suggested it in the first place (Novogratz, 2019).

Going forward with the reorganization would have invalidated legitimate transactions being verified over the course of an entire day (Coin Guides, 2019).

In the end, Binance took on the loss themselves (worth over $40 million at the time) in order to protect clients' investments. Binance counted the loss of 2 percent of their Bitcoin holdings to be a fair price to pay in exchange for learning a valuable lesson about trust and security on the Bitcoin network.

How Bitcoin Democratizes Money

Can Bitcoin really be considered decentralized if the head of one exchange can decide to undo the blockchain? Well, anyone can add, change, or take away from the Bitcoin code. It's all posted publicly on GitHub. But if the community outright rejects your crazy coding changes, then you accomplished nothing other than wasting your own time.

Just because Satoshi wanted to create a system built on verification over trust doesn't mean some trust is not required. In fact, the reason the value of Bitcoin was so low in the early days was because of the fact most people did not trust it yet. Only as the public has begun to trust Bitcoin has its value skyrocketed along with a level of trust.

If one exchange had the power to rewrite the history of the blockchain in order to mitigate its own financial losses, then trust in Bitcoin would collapse overnight. But as long as there are so many exchanges, and a majority of BTC holdings are not concentrated in one, then the Bitcoin network remains a democracy.

When you consider the Binance hack was only the *sixth* largest cryptocurrency exchange hack (Coin Guides, 2019), eroding the public's trust in blockchain just to cover a 2 percent loss of one company's profits would be most unwise.

In another deleted post, the head of Binance accepted his company's loss: "To put this to bed, [re-org] is not possible. Bitcoin ledger is the most immutable ledger on the planet" (Coin Guides, 2019).

Chapter 5

Understanding the Value of Bitcoin

What Drives Bitcoin's Value?

Not everyone in this world is sold on cryptocurrency as a sound investment. There will always be critics and doubters in the moment; only hindsight will prove who was right in the end. So what answer can we give to those who believe Bitcoin is nothing more than a "bubble"?

The populace at large saw the value of Bitcoin shoot up to nearly $70,000 in 2021, and eventually they watched it deflate to its current value of around $30,000. The public is not informed regarding halving events. Therefore they assume something is amiss and are reluctant to invest.

People like Max Keiser were able to predict Bitcoin would reach $60,000 and even predicted the year in which it would do so. They were able to make such accurate predictions regarding Bitcoin's price not because they are prophets, but because they know the mining reward is halved each time 1 percent of the total number of Bitcoin is mined, and this causes a temporary spike in value, as per the laws of supply and demand. If only those who scoff at $30,000 Bitcoin in 2023 knew at one point in 2020 its value was little more than a mere $10,000.

Why Bitcoin Early Adopters Win

Michael Saylor (co-founder of mobile software and cloud service company MicroStrategy) compares early investors in Bitcoin to those who purchased land in New York City in the seventeenth and eighteenth century (Savvy Finance, 2023, 01:10). You see, New York City predates the signing of the Declaration of Independence by over a hundred years.

Saylor imagines some people in 1776 must have been dissuaded from buying land in the city when they thought about how people in the early 1600s likely purchased their lots for pocket change compared to the prices people had to pay in 1776 New York. Some very early adopters may have gotten theirs *for free.* Bitcoin was also given away for free in the early days (Andresen, 2010).

In the same way, you may feel like you've waited too long to get on the Bitcoin train. But think about what will happen if you wait any longer. Yes, those early adopters who got Bitcoin for $1 or less are probably millionaires now. But if you keep waiting, you will end up with the same regrets as those people who turned down investing in a plot of New York City in 1776. Imagine how much their heirs are charging for rent now!

Is Bitcoin a Passing Fad?

Take Paul Krugman, for example. Even a Nobel Prize–winning economist like him has made wildly inaccurate predictions—like in 1998 when he said the growth of the internet would "slow drastically" and that its economic impact would be "no greater than the fax machine's" (Krugman, 1998).

Keep in mind that in 1998 when he wrote that article, 280 million people were online (Ritchie et al., 2023).

By 2018, that number had swollen to 4.7 *billion* people online. In that year, this same economist offered another prediction, saying, "Once the dream of a blockchained future dies, the disappointment will probably collapse the whole thing" (Krugman, 2018). He envisioned a future where Bitcoin would "remain in use mainly for black market transactions and tax evasion."

Wow, that sure sounds biased. In 2020, Visual Objects conducted a survey, which PRNewswire published in an article under the headline "Nearly One-Third of People Believe Cryptocurrency Is Used Primarily for Illegal Purchases, but Actual Purchases May Be More Boring."

The article goes on to say that of the over nine hundred people surveyed, the second most common answer after "stocks" was "illegal items." The data suggested, however, "cryptocurrency is used for everyday purchases more than the general public believes" (Visual Objects, 2020).

I suppose Krugman perhaps isn't aware blockchain technology is truly a revolution and is used for more than just Bitcoin. In fact, just one year after Krugman announced the death of blockchain, Deloitte surveyed over 1,300 senior executives of multimillion-dollar companies from over ten countries around the world. Over 50 percent of those executives said blockchain was a "critical priority" for their company, and it was one of their top five company priorities (Deloitte Insights, 2019).

The World Economic Forum has stated that "wide-scale adoption" of blockchain will increase gross domestic product worldwide by 5 percent and trade by 15 percent (Blount, 2019). IBM touts blockchain's ability to prevent counterfeiting in the pharmaceutical industry and revolutionize auto supply chains (IBM, 2022). Walmart boasts of their robust use of blockchain in various countries, utilizing it to track all of the many food items transported throughout their worldwide network (Sristy, 2021).

We could go on and on, but rest assured, blockchain is revolutionizing industry after industry, and it's not going to slow down, no matter what Krugman says. And when blockchain goes to the top, Bitcoin will go to the top with it. Missing out on Bitcoin now will be remembered in history along with other investment oversights, such as when Blockbuster Video passed up an outright buyout of Netflix for only $50 million (a company now worth $230 billion). Krugman made a bad call on the internet in 1998, and he is calling it wrong on blockchain now.

How Bitcoin Trumps the Dollar

Bitcoin Magazine recently reported the market capitalization of Bitcoin had topped more than $1 trillion dollars (Brunell, 2023). I wonder what the market cap for Bitcoin would have been the day Satoshi released his white paper? Hmm . . . maybe *zero* dollars?

Bitcoin has gone from a humble idea floating in the head of an anonymous programmer to a "legitimate store of wealth" (Novogratz, 2019), with a market cap that currently rivals that of Exxon Mobil, Johnson & Johnson, JP Morgan Chase, and silver (Infinite Market

Cap, 2023). By the time the next halving event occurs, I believe we'll see its resting market cap rival that of Alphabet (Google), Apple, and Microsoft.

You don't know what you've got till it's gone. Ask Laszlo Hanyecz, who confessed to having spent 100,000 BTC on pizzas in 2010, when Bitcoin was worth less than a dollar (Sparks, 2021).

If we could go back in time, we'd all be able to be better investors. That's why maybe we should go easy on Krugman. It's easy to make the right call in hindsight, but successful investors are the ones who can make the right call in the moment.

Evidence is not proof, but when a deluge of evidence rises, a certain point is reached when those who are still not convinced cannot be sympathized with. The people in 1776 who missed out should have assessed New York City as the most successful city in North America, and should have gone all in on riding that wave of opportunity. Instead, they told themselves, "It's a bubble," or "I waited too long."

Since 1971, inflation and the cost of living in the United States have been out of control and show no signs of stopping. The average cost of purchasing a home back then was $24,000; today it is $390,000. Adjusted for inflation, that's $193,000 vs. $390,000: basically double the price for the privilege of not living on the streets (PK, 2023).

The rising value of Bitcoin, however, counteracts the fall of the dollar. Yes, in 2010 one man spent 100,000 BTC on pizza, but for the nearly three billion dollars that's worth in 2023, you could buy up a whole block of New York City pizza joints!

How Governments Destroy Money and How Bitcoin Saves It

Shortly after the firestorm of economic devastation of 1971 began, economist Friedrich Hayek wrote a daring manifesto on monetary revolution, entitled *The Denationalization of Money*. Much like Satoshi releasing his paper in response to the 2008 financial crisis, Hayek's treatise was the "equal but opposite reaction" to the nefarious, wealth-eroding actions of the financial powers of his day:

> The causes of waves of unemployment is not "capitalism" but governments denying enterprise the right to produce *good* money. . . . I don't believe we shall ever have a good money again before we take the thing *out of the hands of government*; that is, we can't take them violently out of the hands of government: all we can do is by some sly roundabout way introduce *something they can't stop*. . . . Governments have at all times had a strong interest in persuading the public that the right to issue money belongs exclusively to them. . . . Governments have become wholly inadequate for the task and, it can be said without qualifications, have incessantly and everywhere abused their trust to defraud the people. . . . The government monopoly of the issue of money was bad enough so long as metallic money predominated. But it became an unrelieved calamity since paper money. . . . A money deliberately controlled in supply by an agency whose self-interest forced it to satisfy the wishes of the *users* might be the best (Hayek, 1976).

The Mises Institute called the book a "most radical case for the complete privatization of money" (Mises Institute, 2014). They summarize the argument of this Nobel Prize–winning economist as "completely abandoning government attempts to reform money." Hayek's vision of an ideal economy was one where only the free market itself decides on its currency of choice.

Outsiders to Bitcoin look at the volatility of its price and get cold feet. Most of them don't spend much time thinking about the fact the average inflation rate of the US dollar from the 1960s until now is almost 4 percent per year (*Inflation Rates in the United States of America*, 2023). That's 4 percent of your money disappearing every year! Storing your wealth in paper fiat is like saving water in a bucket with holes in it!

Contrarily, Bitcoin's purchasing power is destined to climb to new heights. Whenever a halving event occurs, scarcity (a prime driver of value) is doubled as the mining reward is halved. Bitcoin then enters the headlines of mainstream publications again, and the public becomes interested in the peak price. But as the price plateaus (albeit to a higher resting price than before), the public loses interest again, because the average person might not know about halving events or even be aware Bitcoin mining exists.

If you are feeling skittish because of Bitcoin price fluctuations, take a closer look at the real numbers. On the day of the first halving event, 1 BTC was worth $12; five months later, it was worth $127. With the fourth halving event expected to take place in 2024, the price of one Bitcoin currently sits at nearly $30,000 (Roots, 2020).

Eighty percent of all Bitcoin that will ever exist has already been mined. When the mines are empty, the world will go into a frenzy trying to get their hands on as much of the coin as possible. The price then will rise to never-before-seen heights.

One simple statistic quickly silences the Bitcoin naysayers: no asset has reached a $1 trillion market cap faster than Bitcoin. It took Microsoft forty-four years, Apple forty-two, Amazon twenty-four, and Google twenty-one, but it only took Bitcoin twelve years to achieve this milestone (Ali, 2021). That's one humble, anonymous inventor and a small band of guerilla programmers outsmarting all the titans of technology and business.

Contrasting the hyperinflation that has eroded the standard of living of many countries around the world, Bitcoin has stood the test of time where fiat currencies have consistently failed. How many times will the governments of the world repeat the same experiment only to see it fail? Could it be the elite are more concerned with enriching themselves than ensuring prosperity for the people? As Friedrich Hayek wrote in *The Road to Serfdom*, "Once you admit the individual is merely a means to serve the ends of the higher entity called society or the nation, most of those features of totalitarianism which horrify us follow of necessity" (Hayek, 2023).

In the Hemingway novel *The Sun Also Rises,* one character asks another how he went bankrupt. His answer: "Gradually, then suddenly." The same can happen to a nation when hyperinflation of its currency occurs. Think about the death of arcades and the value of a quarter dollar, or the fate of dollar stores (previous generations enjoyed shopping at *penny* stores). As *Bitcoin Magazine* put it: hyperinflation "muddies people's ability to make economic decisions. It gets harder to know how much something 'costs', [or] if a business is making a real profit" (Book, 2023).

The United States Bureau of Engraving & Printing prints seven to nine billion Federal Reserve notes per year, of differing denominations (Federal Reserve, 2022). Now compare that with the fact there will only ever be 21 million BTC, and you've got a surefire way to beat inflation.

I trust by now you are convinced of the privacy, security, and lasting value of Bitcoin. Rest assured it can bring you and your loved ones the financial freedom we all desire. In the next chapter, we will discuss how you can *buy and secure* Bitcoin, criteria for choosing the best *wallet*, and how to protect yourself from scams.

Chapter 6

How to Buy and Store Bitcoin

Where Can I Buy Bitcoin?

We've spent a lot of time covering *why* you should procure Bitcoin if you care about the financial security of yourself and your loved ones. Now let's get into exactly *how* you can make it happen. You will encounter lots of new terminology, and there are seemingly endless options, but it's nothing to be overwhelmed by. Let's simplify the process.

If you want to reap the full rewards of Bitcoin success, you will definitely want to get involved in mining once you feel comfortable. We'll cover that in the next chapter.

The route most people take at first is through trading. Similar to buying stocks in a public company, you will be trading your nation's local currency for the cryptocurrency of your choice. Bitcoin is your best option by far. We'll explain in a little while why the other cryptocurrencies are not as favorable.

Bitcoin is traded on *exchanges*. Most newcomers to the world of crypto get started with a centralized exchange (CEX), but for those who are ready for a more advanced experience, there are decentralized exchanges (DEXs) as well.

A centralized exchange is actually a trusted third party, so it may seem to go against Satoshi's vision at first, but the important thing to remember is there are pros and cons to most things in life. Without an intermediary, many people (who perhaps are not tech savvy) might miss out on the opportunities Bitcoin would otherwise afford them.

You see, any crypto you hold (especially Bitcoin) is a *high-value target* for hackers and thieves. Cryptocurrency is not like paper money—you can't carry it in your pocket or lock it in a safe. It is always stored on the blockchain. What you are tasked with protecting is the private keys to the address where the crypto is stored.

Leaving those exposed to the eyes of strangers on the internet (or in real life) is about as smart as leaving your dog in the house with a juicy red steak on your plate and expecting it to still be there when you come back. In the same way you wouldn't leave your wallet on the dashboard of your car with your windows down while you're swimming at the beach, you shouldn't leave your private keys where they can be intercepted by unseen hackers on the internet (who are getting smarter every day).

This is where using an exchange can save you. These are large corporations who *mostly* know what they are doing. If their customers stand to lose lots of money, then they also stand to lose with them. It's not like the Federal Reserve is going to print more Bitcoin off to insure exchanges!

On a certain level, cryptocurrency advocates are in this together. Because when it comes to blockchain, we all stand to do better when the price of Bitcoin goes up. And if the hackers are in control, faith in Bitcoin goes down, and eventually we all lose.

Having an exchange can be quite useful when you are first dipping your feet in to test the waters. Remember the Binance hack we covered earlier? Well, Binance (the largest cryptocurrency exchange by far) had their own fund saved up to cover clients' losses in the event of an emergency. This fund was used to protect the $40 million of Bitcoin stolen by hackers (due to the fault of the exchange's flawed security).

Binance took on the loss themselves, instead of attempting to fork the blockchain: a move which protected Bitcoin's price and reputation. This is just one example of how having a trusted third party such as an exchange could come in handy for Bitcoin amateurs.

What Are Altcoins?

While we're on the topic of reorganizing the blockchain, let's talk about Ethereum. This, along with Dogecoin and a myriad of other cryptocurrencies, are referred to as *altcoins*.

When the Bitcoin community *wisely* decided against forking the blockchain, they had a precedent to reference in their decision: the splitting of Ethereum's blockchain. You see, Ethereum had been hacked in the past, and since this altcoin was still in its early days, they decided to basically hit "undo" on what the hackers had managed to pull off. But some users did not want to be a part of this change, and so Ethereum Classic was born (a separate blockchain).

In practice, this looks like the following: "ETC and ETH blockchains included identical past blocks, but they diverged going forward" (Ashmore, 2023). Even though Ethereum has historically been the second most valuable altcoin, its value is still a mere fraction of Bitcoin's, and Ethereum Classic's price is only a tiny fraction of Ethereum's.

So is it worth investing in altcoins? While you might be able to reap a small profit from certain ones over time, it's important to note they are referred to as "alt" coins because they are destined to always live in the shadow of Bitcoin's success. This is because they are all inspired by Satoshi's white paper and are, by definition, *imitations* of the real thing.

While there may be hundreds of thousands of athletes aspiring to "be like Mike," there is only one Michael Jordan. There are over one hundred altcoins now, and because Satoshi's design, along with the resulting Bitcoin code, is open-source and not patented, there will always be more and more of them. But all their values are not even comparable to Bitcoin's. The original is still the best—by far!

How to Choose the Right Bitcoin Exchange

If you're serious about making money with Bitcoin, eventually you will find yourself mining your own and storing your private keys in a secure *wallet* offline. But first let's take you through it in baby steps.

Crypto exchanges function in a very similar manner to stock exchanges. Whether in your web browser or through their dedicated mobile applications, you'll be able to place market orders or limit orders on the cryptocurrency of your choice at any time.

One key difference to note from stock market exchanges is there is no closing time: 24/7/365 you will be able to convert your nation's inflated fiat currency into BTC. Another difference is by purchasing cryptocurrency, you are not becoming partial owner of any company.

Lastly, while many companies can issue more shares whenever they need more funding, there is never going to be more than 21 million Bitcoin (Cointree, 2021).

A good or bad exchange can make or break your Bitcoin investments. There are many factors involved in choosing a good one. Before we discuss the qualities used to identify an ideal exchange, let's briefly look at an instance of a poor one.

If you read any type of news, you've probably heard about the company FTX. This cryptocurrency exchange made the same mistake that many financial institutions before it also made: taking consumers' funds and spending them without ensuring enough capital was kept on hand to cover withdrawals.

When the public (including big names in the crypto space) began to wise up to the sorry state of the company, they began to sell. Binance backed out of an acquisition deal. Soon FTX had to freeze withdrawals due to a lack of available funds. They then declared bankruptcy, and the CEO was arrested and sent to jail.

Maxine Waters, a Democrat Representative from California, commented on the matter: "The fall of FTX has posed tremendous harm to over one million users, many of whom were everyday people who invested their hard-earned savings into the FTX cryptocurrency exchange, only to watch it all disappear within a matter of seconds."

ABC News reported how the replacement CEO, John Ray (the same person who guided Enron through their well-publicized bankruptcy case), stated it was the worst failure of corporate controls he had ever seen, worse than Enron, describing it as "the concentration of control in the hands of a very small group of inexperienced, unsophisticated, and potentially compromised individuals." The former CEO, Sam Bankman-Fried, was charged by the SEC with defrauding its investors (Zahn, 2022).

What Are Custodial and Non-Custodial Exchanges?

Obviously, no one wants to end up having their savings sabotaged by tragic events like these, so in this chapter you're going to acquire the knowledge you need to safely procure and protect your own Bitcoin stash. As long as you have the right set of knowledge, your investments will be safe.

From choosing the best exchange to choosing the best wallet to store your private keys offline, you will be equipped with a foolproof battle plan to secure your own personal wealth with Bitcoin. It is very sad how people have lost their investments by putting too much trust in a third party, but don't let their mistakes dissuade you from investing in Bitcoin with confidence.

To avoid ending up with the same fate as those whose funds were swallowed up by FTX, it's a necessity to learn how to store your private keys offline. There are layers and layers of security you can add to your keys with wallets.

First, you've got to make sure the exchange you choose allows you to have access to your keys. This is arguably the most important criterion to consider when selecting a crypto exchange. If you leave your keys in the custody of an exchange, then you will lose your Bitcoin if the company goes out of business, if you are locked out due to violating their terms of use, or if you forget your login credentials.

Exchanges not allowing private ownership of keys are called *custodial* exchanges. Why would anyone in their right mind use one of these? Well, doing so is certainly a risk, so you should never store large amounts of Bitcoin with such a service, nor should you keep it there long. Some minor benefits may exist, however, such as potentially competitive transaction fees.

While many who jump onto such platforms may be newcomers who aren't informed regarding private key custody, some advanced Bitcoin users still recommend this type of exchange. Why? One reason is ease of use.

For newcomers in the crypto space or those who are technologically illiterate, a simpler service just feels right. Being personally responsible for the custody of one's own keys can be intimidating. As Paul Puey from Edge Wallet explains, "Human error has been a huge amount of the security pitfalls in self-custody" (Crypto Tips, 2022, 11:29).

If you attempt to handle your keys yourself and make a mistake, there's nothing you can do. This can include taking a picture of your key with your internet-connected smartphone, leaving your hardware wallet in your pocket while washing your pants, putting your keys on what you thought was a software wallet but was malware in disguise, or sending your keys in an email response to someone you thought was a customer service agent of the wallet or exchange you use.

Every single one of these scenarios has led to at least one person losing Bitcoin forever. This is why some people elect to let the big buys handle it and just trust the exchange to provide all the security.

Now perhaps you can see why, when surveyed, 75 percent of those who don't own any crypto say "lack of knowledge" is the reason they've never invested (Thubron, 2021). But don't you worry, because we're going to make it the easiest thing to understand.

What Is a Decentralized Exchange?

Before we get into wallets, let's first briefly cover another type of exchange. Whereas a centralized exchange (or CEX) acts as an intermediary, connecting buyers and sellers, a decentralized exchange (or DEX) is truly peer-to-peer.

Decentralized cryptocurrency exchanges rely on *smart contracts*. This means there is no need for trust in any third party. The code of the contract is executed when the set criteria are met and crypto is exchanged directly between two individuals (Crypto Tips, 2023, 1:45).

DEXs should be an option for intermediates and experts in crypto. Because you are directly trading assets with unknown people over the internet, the risk is certainly higher than if you went through a CEX, which would protect you against fraud and store your keys for you. Though CEXs aren't perfect either, as we have seen.

In a certain sense, however, DEXs are more secure, since the cryptoassets are transferred directly to your wallet, the keys of which you will be in direct custody of. But there is still much risk overall when using a DEX. Bitcoin.com weighs in on the matter:

By far the biggest barrier to using DEXs is the UI/UX difficulty. It is confusing and hard to get cryptoassets into a wallet, and then navigate the user interfaces of most DEXs. There's a lot of up-front learning involved before you will be able to execute a single trade. . . . Because anyone can add a cryptoasset to a DEX, scams are ever present. Any legitimate project will spawn dozens of scam projects with the same name or slightly different names to try and trick you into swapping your cryptoassets (Bitcoin.com, 2022).

So why would anyone want to use a DEX if the risk is so high? One such reason is all of the increasingly complex hoops CEXs are forcing users to jump through in order to use their services. These requirements are referred to within the crypto community as "KYC."

What Is KYC?

KYC stands for *know your customer*. One principle of Bitcoin from the beginning has been anonymity. After all, we still don't know who Satoshi is.

KYC is a creeping policy shift being implemented by many exchanges and even some wallet providers. This is a policy where the service you are using wants to know maybe a little more about you than you'd like to share.

Tayler McCracken of The Coin Bureau shares his experience with KYC: "When I first started using Binance, I could do it without providing any information at all; it was quick and easy. However, over time, KYC requirements progressed, and I now feel like I have had to provide them with my entire life story, an autobiography, a list of my likes and dislikes, my favourite colour and name of my first pet" (McCracken, 2022).

The reason cryptocurrency services are beginning to require more and more information about their users is because of new regulations being passed in different parts of the world, which are aimed at curbing money-laundering schemes. Some exchanges give advance notice, so those who do not wish to be identified can transfer their BTC beforehand, from one exchange to another, before the new requirements take effect. In the case of Binance, however, the policy change took immediate effect.

Some KYC policies require a picture of a government-issued ID, along with a photograph of the user's face. What if you don't have an ID or it is expired? This may only affect a minority of people in first-world countries today, but for many people in less developed parts of the world, these heightened requirements might be seen as unnecessary barriers to entry into the world of crypto.

The World Bank reports that 850 million people "do not have official identification—primarily people in lower-income countries and marginalized and vulnerable groups" (The World Bank, 2018). This is largely due to documentary requirements, distance of the nearest registration center, and inability to pay associated fees. For people in low-income nations who find themselves in situations like these, discovering peer-to-peer Bitcoin trading could be like striking gold.

What Is a Bitcoin Wallet?

I've been tepid, I've been timid when Max Keiser tried to give me 10,000 Bitcoin and I couldn't figure out how to put a digital wallet on my Apple laptop, so that's a big train that I missed (Jones, 2021, 03:04).

A *Bitcoin wallet* is a means of keeping the private keys to your Bitcoin address secure from unwanted access. It can refer to several different things, such as a software service or hardware device.

It's important to note that people often use the terms "wallet address" and "Bitcoin address" interchangeably. Technically speaking, *Bitcoin address* is the official term. The amount of BTC you hold is always stored on the blockchain—never in any app or hardware-based wallet. Where they are located on the blockchain is officially known as your Bitcoin address, though many refer to it as their *wallet address*.

Blockchain technology is a revolutionary leap in software engineering, so its concepts can be lost on those who aren't familiar with such fields. Since Bitcoin was designed for use by the common man, concepts are named using terms such as *mining* or *wallet* from fields that more people are familiar with.

Wallets, in regard to Bitcoin, do not actually store your currency, but in the experience of the user, the process may feel quite similar. What the wallet actually stores is your public keys (your addresses on the blockchain) and corresponding private keys (which give you access to perform transactions using said Bitcoin addresses on the blockchain).

Wallets can come in the form of software, accessed through a web browser or mobile phone application. These software solutions will simplify the process of transacting in Bitcoin and provide easy-to-use security for private keys. The value shown to the user on screen will be a combined value of all his Bitcoin addresses. Transactions can be made using multiple addresses simultaneously.

Remember, software wallets are internet connected. This leaves keys potentially vulnerable to compromise. Offline storage of keys in a hardware-based wallet can provide much greater security.

Software wallets are used by many, however, due to their simplicity. This is because as human beings, we are biased towards colorful, flashy user interfaces. We also tend to be lazy by nature and favor the speedy access to our coins software wallets provide.

There is also a certain layer of discretion software wallets allow. If one were to try to get through an airport with $100,000 USD in his suitcase, he would almost certainly get stopped. Whether he did something wrong does not matter; the policy of governments around the world is to stop and interrogate anyone transporting large amounts of currency (and often confiscate it).

A Bitcoin hardware wallet device is less conspicuous than a suitcase full of dollars or euros, but could still potentially raise some eyebrows. An app on your phone, however, will go entirely unnoticed.

Hardware wallets are strongly recommended for long-term storage, but for a week in Venice, a software wallet app might be your best friend. Only store on it the amount of BTC you are likely to need for the trip.

It is recommended to use a mobile phone application rather than a web browser on a desktop, for added security. This is because mobile phone operating systems have historically been better at storing each application's data in "sandboxed" storage.

Apple defines sandboxing as such:

> All third-party apps are "sandboxed," so they are restricted from accessing files stored by other apps or from making changes to the device. Sandboxing is designed to prevent apps from gathering or modifying information stored by other apps. . . . Unnecessary tools, such as remote login services, aren't included in the system software, and APIs don't allow apps to escalate their own privileges to modify other apps or iOS and iPadOS (Apple Inc., 2021).

Desktop operating systems are from an earlier time and have been slow to catch up to mobile OS such as Apple's iOS. For example, mobile operating systems are encrypted by default.

iOS is more secure than other mobile operating systems since it does not allow arbitrary installation of software; all software must be installed through the manufacturer's own vetted storefront, where every application is scanned for malware and personally approved by a human being at some point in the process. Contrarily, Android OS does allow for easy opting in to arbitrary software installation, but you can simply leave the setting in its default off position.

With this in mind, it's important to note there are malware applications out there, as well as fraudulent web sites, pretending to be software wallets for your Bitcoin, but in fact are only phishing operations which bad actors have set up to trick you into revealing your private keys.

So if you're going to use a software wallet, make sure it's from a reputable company. Make sure you obtain the software from the corresponding storefront of your mobile OS provider.

One great app, and the one I use for sending and receiving Bitcoin, is Cash App. It encrypts your data, is free to install, and is owned by the same people who own Square, which is a very popular point of sale option for a large and growing number of businesses, such as local cafés, concert merchandise tables, and even farmers markets.

They recently filed for a patent related to accepting cryptocurrency as payment directly on their Square POS devices. Maybe one day soon you'll find yourself spending Bitcoin directly at many places you never thought possible.

Can I Switch Software Wallets after Setting One Up?

What happens if you already set up a software wallet but later decide on one you like better? No worries, just make sure you choose a software wallet supporting BIP39, Bitcoin Improvement Proposal 39.

The BIP program is a method of democratizing future implementation of code improvements to the Bitcoin protocol. BIP39, in particular, standardizes "how cryptocurrency wallets generate mnemonic phrases and convert them into binary seeds, which can be used to create deterministic wallets" (ABECOIN, 2022, 2:20).

Mnemonic phrases are passphrases that are easier to memorize, usually consisting of twelve to twenty-four words. Having wallets standardize how they implement such passphrases means you won't get locked out of your funds if a software wallet provider goes out of business, is shut down by government order, stops supporting your cryptoasset of choice (as was the case with Coinbase Wallet and XRP), or implements a sudden change in KYC you cannot or choose not to adhere to for one reason or another.

To reiterate: your Bitcoin is always stored *on the blockchain*, and the wallet holds your keys. So simply choose a new software wallet supporting BIP39 (currently Exodus, Mycelium, Samourai, Coinomi, BlueWallet, Wasabi, Phoenix, and Trust), and you'll be able to import your old wallet during the setup process (ABECOIN, 2022, 3:10). As long as you have your phrase, it couldn't be easier.

Some *hardware* wallets also support BIP39, such as Trezor, Ledger, and COLDCARD. Let's learn how to choose the best one.

What Is the Difference Between Hot and Cold Bitcoin Storage?

Software wallets are referred to as "hot" storage. When using a software wallet, your Bitcoin is ready to be spent at a moment's notice. But your keys are not stored as securely as they would be on a hardware wallet, since they are stored on an internet-connected device. For large amounts of value, or for Bitcoin you plan to hold for a long period of time, hardware wallets should be considered the optimum solution.

Hardware wallets are referred to as "cold" storage. They are the ideal way to let your BTC lie dormant for long periods of time.

There are many hardware wallet providers to choose from. They all operate in different ways and have different user interfaces. One of the most popular providers is Trezor. I personally use a Trezor Model T wallet and have experienced no issues. Trezor is a great option because they are a private company and are not beholden to the demands of investors. As stated on their own web page regarding their stance on this matter:

> Trezor is an independent company and we are not bound to any outside investment. We do not participate in venture capital funding because we do not want to compromise the security of our product. Making decisions without external influence allows us to be completely transparent as we focus on supporting Bitcoin's development (Trezor, 2023).

Contrast Trezor with the company Ledger, which does seek investment. With Trezor wallets, you only have to pay once, whereas Ledger rolled out a monthly subscription service. More than just a few Bitcoin advocates have sounded alarms over this service, not just because it was likely envisioned as a recurring revenue stream to appease investors, but because it sends your passphrases over the internet.

This seems to go against the entire purpose of hardware wallets, which is to store your private Bitcoin information in a device not needing to connect to the internet. If you opt in to this service, your data will be encrypted, then divided into separate "shards," which will then be sent out to separate companies for storage in "the cloud" (i.e., someone else's computer).

The marketed demographic for this service is those who can't remember their passphrases, as if you do forget your passphrases, you can be locked out of potentially millions of dollars!

So there will be people who opt to use this service, but many Bitcoin gurus (including software engineers) have firmly cautioned against it.

One reason for this consternation is the fact Ledger previously suffered a data breach in which a million of its users' email addresses were leaked (Lee, 2023, 0:15). Another reason is the companies tasked with storing customers' "shards" of data exist under different jurisdictions, including the United States, the United Kingdom, and the European Union (Lee, 2023, 2:35). This means Ledger users might be forced to comply with any new regulation passed in such territories.

The benefit of a cloud-based service like this would be to the elderly or anyone who may have a neurodegenerative disease, or anyone who may have a poor memory in general. If you get locked out of your Bitcoin address due to your own human error, then no one is coming to save you. If you signed up for Ledger Recover previously, then you will certainly not regret such a decision. It is an opt-in program, but some users are wary about these lines of code even existing in their wallets—lines of code designed to upload their passphrases to third parties in other countries.

How Can I Keep My Wallet Secure?

As humans, we like to see and touch things here in the third dimension, so having a physical device to hold in our hands is a more comfortable experience to us, as we are used to carrying around billfolds or pocketbooks with our paper money and credit cards.

You probably wouldn't like to empty the contents of your wallet and show it to everyone on the internet. In the same way, your hardware wallet should be kept disconnected from the internet as much as possible.

Some wallets come with Bluetooth technology for convenient viewing and syncing of your data from your smartphone. This is, of course, a short-range risk.

If you are in a crowded area like a school dormitory or shopping mall, it would be wise to refrain from using such a feature. If your house is surrounded by acres of woods, then maybe you'll find the convenience outweighs any potential risk.

Even though they are called "hardware" wallets, there is a software component. Not only is there the software that runs locally on the device (referred to as "firmware"), but there is also a program you will run on your computer, which will help you view all of your data using a more comfortable user interface: like Trezor Suite, for example.

Both Trezor Suite and the firmware of Trezor devices are open-source. Be sure to install your software and its updates from the official websites of these companies to ensure you're not being tricked into installing a build of the software or firmware that's been tampered with.

What these devices do is store the public and private keys to your Bitcoin address in an encrypted form. Remember: even though your hardware wallet is disconnected from the internet, all of your Bitcoin is located on the blockchain itself.

Since the blockchain is public, if you control a Bitcoin address with lots of BTC in it, you could become a high-value target for hackers.

How Do I Set Up My Hardware Wallet?

While nothing in life is perfect, offline cold storage of your private keys is the *best* solution for keeping your BTC secure. For the tech savvy, setting up a hardware wallet like a Trezor or COLDCARD could be a really fun experience. But even if you feel intimidated by it, don't worry: we're going to go through every step of the process here.

Let's use the Trezor Model T as an example. The first thing you'll want to do is ensure the holographic sticker seal has not been tampered with in any way. If it looks torn or unofficial, send it back. This is especially true if you bought it from eBay or Craigslist, which is in itself a big mistake. Only buy from the official Trezor shop or one of their "trusted resellers."

The next thing you'll want to do is plug your wallet device into your computer's USB port, then download and install the Trezor Suite desktop application from the official source: trezor.io/start. To ensure the best security, it is advised not to use the web browser suite, since it adds more potential for compromise, such as an expired SSL certificate, an out-of-date browser, or a third-party browser extension that may contain malware.

Now you will choose your firmware. There is a universal version and a BTC-only version. Do as you like (you can change it in the future). Once the firmware is finished installing, you'll have the option to set up a new wallet or recover an existing one.

I would recommend wiping your wallet after we complete the following steps, for the purpose of testing the recovery option. This is to ensure everything is *fully* working as it should and to ensure the passphrases you wrote down are the same *100 percent exact* thing you entered into the device.

The reason for this is it would not be wise to dump all your BTC into something you're not sure can be recovered. What if you HODL (hold on for dear life) for ten years, only to discover your physical wallet went faulty on you and you made a mistake while writing down your recovery phrase? Taking this extra step will make sure it doesn't happen to you.

For now, let's choose a backup option. In the current firmware, you'll have two options: Standard or Shamir. The Standard option will have you create a list of words to write down and store securely, which is what most people choose. The Shamir option will have you create several lists of words, which it would be wise to store in separate locations.

Which option you choose here is up to you. While one option may seem more secure, remember: if you lock yourself out by making access too complex, then all your security is for nothing in the end. Human error has brought many to this fate, and thus there are some Bitcoins on the blockchain that may be lost forever.

So if you're just starting out with cryptocurrency, choosing the standard option is fine. Don't worry, because by purchasing a Trezor

Model T, you're already in an elite club of Bitcoin insiders. You're doing better than most to keep your Bitcoin secure.

Once you select your type, you'll have to hit the green button on the touch screen to confirm. The desktop application will have you confirm you have read the disclaimers about not sharing your phrases with anyone online or offline. You can then write down the words which are randomly generated on the device's screen.

Secure storage options exist for your paper backup, such as CryptoTag Zeus Titanium Seed Storage. Maybe "bulletproof" just makes for good marketing, but finding something fireproof and waterproof is a great idea.

Before you move on, make sure you did not make any spelling mistake or any other deviation from the displayed phrases on the device's screen. The device will take you through a pop quiz to make sure you wrote everything down correctly, so simply choose the correct responses to continue.

Now return to the desktop application in order to set up a PIN. You will also see an option to enable TOR VPN for added security. The only downside to VPN is slightly longer loading time, so I'd recommend you enable it.

You can now name your device if you wish to. After this, you will be given the option of creating a standard wallet or a hidden wallet. This part might seem confusing at first. What you are being given here is the option to create virtually unlimited "wallets" on your wallet hardware device, which will only be shown to the person who knows the secret passphrase.

This hidden wallet will give you "plausible deniability" (e.g., you can show a portion of your total BTC holdings on the screen of the hardware wallet, while larger balances remain hidden in secret). This could prove to be a lifesaver if you are ever robbed. If the screen shows $25 in BTC, then you can drain the public wallet when asked, while the remainder of your holdings exists in hidden wallets.

You are 100 percent going to want to write down the secret passphrases to your hidden wallets, if you elect to create some. Make *triple sure* every single character is correct. Do not share this code with anyone. Keep it locked away from the gaze of others.

You can browse forums such as Reddit and find dozens of stories of people who locked themselves out of their hidden wallets after forgetting their secret passphrase or writing it down incorrectly. The longer you make any passphrase, the better, as the difficulty in cracking it grows exponentially with the number of characters or words.

At this point, your wallet is ready to use. If you want to make extra certain that everything is fully secure, you can transfer a tiny amount of BTC to it and then factory reset it. Unplug your Trezor device, then replug it. Then select Recover Wallet to recover everything using your seed phrase.

When it's done, it will ask you to set up your PIN again. Then you should see the same exact balance you transferred before wiping. Now you are all set and have full peace of mind! Keep in mind, things change over time; always consult the latest instructions for your specific device.

Why Randomization Is Important

Another highly secure option is COLDCARD brand wallets (made by Coinkite). I also personally use a COLDCARD wallet to store some of my Bitcoin. Some of them include one hundred tiny dice that you will roll in order to create a truly random seed. This will offer you nothing short of peak security.

Since there is no truly random number in computing, a seed serves as a criterion for the computer to generate a random number. Many people don't understand the importance of actually rolling the dice, and they rush through it by entering a single digit like "5," something common like "777," or something discoverable like a birthday.

Since much wallet firmware is open source, nothing is stopping hackers from analyzing all of the code that goes into determining the "random" numbers generated by your hardware wallet.

If they know your seed and are also familiar with the open-source code, they could potentially end up guessing their way into your wallet. For example: if you are a public figure and chose your birthday as your seed number, then a hacker could crawl your Facebook timeline looking for all those "Happy Birthday" messages.

Humans are terrible at randomness. Let the device do it for you by choosing the twelve- or twenty-four-character option, or else you will actually need to roll one hundred dice and input all the numbers. Otherwise, you could wake up and find your Bitcoin address empty, like one user reported on social media:

About three weeks ago, I had a chunk of CAD disappear off of a COLDCARD MK4. Enough to follow up. Not air gapped, not dice rolled, I just set it up in a hurry before heading out on a Friday night over the summer. I'm pretty sure I button mashed/faked dice rolls for entropy. I threw some [Satoshis] in here and there and kind of forgot about it honestly. . . . Hardware has a great reputation, so I wasn't worried. My mistake though was in the entropy generation. I should have, as Coinkite recommends, either let the device generate the key for me, or done the proper dice roll model—100+ rolls to ensure randomness. I didn't, and a few weeks ago someone was able to break the seed phrase. The MK4 will generate a key for you, or you can roll dice and feed it the numbers for additional randomness. I chose dice roll, and then didn't roll any dice, just button mashed (Canadian Bitcoiners Podcast, 2023).

CHAPTER 7

EARNING PROFIT WITH BITCOIN MINING

How Does Bitcoin Mining Work?

Are you sold on Bitcoin yet? Are ready to go all in on the digital gold rush? Over the years, you've traded your precious time for paper fiat, hemorrhaging value every day. Next, you began protecting those savings by converting them to value-accruing Bitcoin. Now, you are finally ready to join the big leagues and mine some freshly minted Bitcoin of your own. Let's explore the several options available to you at this time and their potential costs and profitability.

We'll start at the bottom of the barrel here. Since not everyone is willing or able to afford dedicated mining equipment, of course the free market has devised ways to lower the barrier of entry. Among these are mining from a web browser, mining from a mobile phone app, and mining using cloud computing. But do these low-cost, beginner-friendly methods stand any chance of being profitable in this highly competitive field? To answer, we first need to explain how mining works.

Bitcoin mining (more specifically, the Bitcoin protocol itself) is the core of decentralized finance (DeFi). In the past, powerful elites fiercely guarded their monopoly over the money supply and "threw the book" at anyone stepping outside of their rules (or even daring to operate in gray zones).

There's a common proverb: "everyone gets his fifteen minutes of fame." Well, thanks to Satoshi's ingenuity, anyone on Earth has the potential to earn his fifteen minutes as a banker. This is accomplished by volunteering the CPU power of your *node* (your computing device) to the verification of transactions.

How this works is the Bitcoin protocol determines an arbitrary number of zeros a hash must start with. The hashes on the Bitcoin network are encoded maps of data using SHA-256. This algorithm scrambles the transactions and other data and spits out something looking like this:

d04b98f48e8f8bcc15c6ae5ac050801cd6dcfd428fb5f9e65c4e16e7807340fa

The Bitcoin protocol randomly decides on a *nonce* (a number of zeros) the hash must start with in order to be accepted. In order to achieve this, one cannot simply add zeros to the start of the hash, but must input arbitrary data into the algorithm along with the transactions and other pertinent data, which will result in an organically generated hash with the correct nonce.

While this may sound like a complex process, rest assured that you don't need to fully understand it to turn a profit with Bitcoin mining. All you need to succeed is the most powerful equipment you can get your hands on, the lowest cost of electricity, and a little bit of luck.

Essentially, what is happening is your node is attempting to guess the correct nonce. If guessed correctly, you win the latest batch of new Bitcoins (6.25 BTC at the moment), and your block is verified and added to the ledger.

The more computationally powerful your device is, the more guesses it can make per second, giving you a greater chance at reaping the highly sought-after reward.

Satoshi and his engineers created a system that increases its difficulty along with the rate of verification. This, along with the halving of mining payouts at every 210,000 mintings, are more than able to make inflation a nonissue in regard to Bitcoin.

Mining is kept secure because the Bitcoin protocol utilizes the Elliptic Curve Digital Signature Algorithm (ECDSA) for signature verification. This ensures no one but the owner of the correct keys can spend the funds at the corresponding address. The specific curve used with this algorithm is Secp256k1. If you enjoy algebra, then you will have fun studying how this specific curve and algorithm make it essentially impossible for an intruder to guess your private key. We won't get too boresome with the technical details here.

All you need to know right now is you can rest assured in the security of the Bitcoin protocol. The hacks we've discussed so far have been perpetrated upon *exchanges* and other companies providing proprietary services to cryptocurrency users: not upon Bitcoin itself or its ledger.

Secp256k1 was published in 2000 by Certicom Research and is used in OpenSSL, as well as in other cryptocurrency networks (Stack Exchange, 2012). It went largely unnoticed and unused until Satoshi and his clever associates scooped it up, and now it has gained a lot of notoriety due to its usefulness in spitting out impossible-to-guess numbers (Bitcoin Wiki, 2019).

It is also praised for its computing efficiency due to it always using numbers that are 256-bit (making them faster for computers to read and store) (MetaMaths, 2021, 5:40).

What Are the Most Affordable Ways to Mine Bitcoin?

Over ten years removed from the dawn of Bitcoin, mining has become a fiercely competitive field. But many people still manage to mine $40,000 worth of BTC per year or more. It's entirely possible, but you must take into account the upfront cost of buying dedicated, high-powered mining computers, as well as a monumental increase in your electric bill.

So are there any cheaper options? As mentioned earlier, there are websites claiming to mine Bitcoin for you through your web browser. Probably all you're going to accomplish on these sites is heavy battery drain and overheating. You might even be giving your sensitive information away to shady companies who will then sell it.

Mobile mining apps are also available. I would not recommend installing these in our present day. Since mining competition has reached unprecedented heights, and since dedicated mining equipment has become relatively affordable, it is, statistically speaking, *practically* impossible for your phone to guess the correct nonce before the army of dedicated mining computers does—though the probability is, in theory, greater than zero.

Then there is cloud mining. Assuming you've found a reputable company and not a scam, what you would be doing here is paying a monthly fee for someone with dedicated miners to participate in the Bitcoin network on your behalf.

Assuming you find any of these services to actually be profitable, the law of supply and demand would have it that word of mouth would spread too quickly, and profitability would disappear shortly thereafter. Think about it: we're essentially talking about signing up for a monthly payment plan in order to get larger checks in the mail than what you send out every month.

This doesn't seem like a lasting business model. Then again, Bitcoin was created in order to turn our understanding of what is possible in the financial world upside down. Who knows? Maybe you'll get lucky and end up making a small profit.

What Is the Most Profitable Method of Bitcoin Mining?

Time is money, and none of us have enough to waste on fruitless endeavors. So when we discuss Bitcoin mining, let's cut straight to the point. If you're going to make a respectable profit relative to your investment, in our present situation, you're going to want to do it through dedicated mining hardware. These are called ASICs.

In the early days, when most people didn't know about Bitcoin mining, the mathematical puzzles to be solved were not as difficult due to a lower hash rate. Back then, you could mine Bitcoin with a simple laptop.

Eventually, you had to get a more powerful gaming computer in order to keep up with the growing competition. But now, ASICs (application specific integrated circuits) have gone down in price and up in power, so you're only going to burn out your traditional PC with unnecessary wear and tear and won't have a chance to earn much in the process if you don't invest in an ASIC.

Trezor created one of the first *mining pools*. These work by giving you power in numbers.

By working as a team, your combined computational power has a higher chance of nabbing the prize—but the profits will be split up according to everyone's level of contribution. You'll be getting paid more frequently this way, but in smaller payouts.

ASIC computers are hard-coded solely for the purpose of cryptocurrency mining, so there is no waste of CPU resources. Their availability has increased steadily, and you can find them on sites like Amazon and eBay.

Keep in mind, these machines put out a lot of noise and heat. They are also power hogs. Depending on where you live, your electric bill may eat into your profits sharply.

You might want to invest in mining storage located in a region with cheaper electric costs. These companies will store your machine, provide maintenance, and foot the electric bill (business rates for power usage are usually lower than residential).

You'll send them your equipment and pay a monthly storage fee, then reap the rewards. This is the preferred setup of many serious miners today. If you fancy yourself an entrepreneur, why not rent a warehouse and start a mining storage business of your own?

Bitcoin Mining and the Environment

There is a vocal subset of people who want to see Bitcoin mining fundamentally altered or decommissioned altogether.

Among these is art activist Benjamin Von Wong, who partnered with Greenpeace to create the "Skull of Satoshi": a large skull-shaped object constructed from circuit boards and computer cables, complete with working smokestacks on top.

Advocates like him want Bitcoin to switch to a proof-of-stake system, which Ethereum now uses. Ethereum's value, however, is only a small fraction of Bitcoin's. Remember, proof-of-work, devised by Adam Back, is the backbone of Bitcoin security. It is the nuts and bolts of transaction verification.

Does proof-of-stake provide the security needed for a DeFi system in which the people themselves are their own bankers? The Bitcoin protocol (built upon Back's proof-of-work function) is what objectively decides who gets to be a temporary banker for the next set of transactions. It would not be wise to tamper with it. Security should be the *only* factor in determining what consensus mechanism governs the verification of an asset reaching the height of a trillion-dollar market cap—not hypothetical warnings of impending doom.

There is a quieter majority who propose mining is actually good for the environment, since miners are shifting heavily to using clean forms of energy such as hydro, wind, and solar. Miners also shut down when there is a shortage of electricity, giving the grid the opportunity to supply essential services.

Many are not aware excess gas from wells is burned off. Bitcoin mining has provided a way to convert this unused energy into prosperity for lower- and middle-class individuals, who might otherwise be commuting into the cities in search of wages.

99Bitcoins adds some insight to the issue:

While there has been a lot of criticism about the amount of energy consumption that Bitcoin mining employs worldwide, there are various arguments against this claim as well. For starters, you could argue that Bitcoin mining uses less resources than the current banking system. If you take into account banks, servers, ATMs, credit card companies, and all other components of the current monetary system, you'll find out that it's much more wasteful than Bitcoin mining, especially when you consider all of the paper used for printing money, and the pollution caused by these institutions. Also, you could say that Bitcoin mining is actually optimizing power consumption around the world. Many mining companies are moving their operations to countries that have an excess of electricity. This means that the use of electricity worldwide is actually becoming more efficient (99Bitcoins, 2018, 13:13).

CHAPTER 8

BITCOIN'S ROLE IN THE GLOBAL ECONOMY

Bitcoin Versus TradFi

Banking without Borders

The Declaration of Independence solemnly admonishes us: changes in governmental systems ought not to be carried out for "light and transient causes." Monetary policies and institutions have traditionally been intertwined with government since time immemorial. Former head of the Federal Reserve Alan Greenspan boasted, "There is no other agency of government that can overrule actions that we [the Federal Reserve] take" (Greenspan, 2008).

Thomas Jefferson specified the reason mankind institutes governments: to secure "life, liberty, and the pursuit of happiness." Jefferson also wrote an escape hatch into the Declaration for times when the people experience "a long train of abuses and usurpations": "whenever any Form of Government becomes destructive of these ends, it is the Right of the People to alter or to abolish it, and to institute new Government . . . to provide new Guards for their future security" (Jefferson, 1776).

As homeless encampments are growing in cities all across the United States, and mom-and-pop shops are disappearing faster than ever, the common people owe it to themselves to adopt a better system of finance.

And it's not just the United States that will benefit. People all around the world are finding tremendous benefits in Bitcoin.

El Salvador, the seventeenth most populous nation, made Bitcoin legal tender in 2021 and created their own government-backed wallet (Foote, 2022). When you take into account Bitcoin transaction fees can be up to 90 percent less expensive than those required by traditional financial institutions (Desjardins & Rao, 2014), people in poorer nations stand to experience the greatest benefit from Bitcoin.

In time, Bitcoin may even prove itself a better guardian of life, liberty, and the pursuit of happiness than the Constitution. Such systems promised people liberty but were hindered by the implementation of fiat currencies.

In the 1800s, libertarian philosopher Lysander Spooner, being part of the second generation of Americans to live under the Constitution, gave his opinion on the effect it and the resulting monetary policies had:

> The writer thinks it proper to say that, in his opinion, the Constitution is no such instrument as it has generally been assumed to be; but that by false interpretations, and naked usurpations, the government has been made in practice a very widely, and almost wholly, different thing from what the Constitution itself purports to authorize. He has heretofore written much, and could write much more, to prove that such is the truth. But whether the Constitution really be one thing, or another, this much is certain—that it has either authorized such a government as we have had, or has been powerless to prevent it (Spooner, 1870).

Since Bitcoin relies on verification over trust, it is able to penetrate the barriers the credit-based system has set up: barriers that tend to function almost as a new caste system in the twenty-first century. Bitcoin doesn't care about who you are, what culture you come from, or what mistakes you may have made in the past. It also doesn't care about how powerful you are in the political hierarchy. It is an equalizer, just as a firearm would be an equalizer for a frail person against an attacker of greater strength.

With Bitcoin, there is no credit check required and no fear of charge-backs. When doing business across international borders, Bitcoin provides "a Stargate-like bridge between our two monetary dimensions . . . a timeless bridge between two different dimensions of wealth" (Joël Valenzuela, 2016).

Rather than private companies such as PayPal or Western Union, who may want to police people's opinions or spy on their activities, DeFi could be better compared to the open internet itself.

How Businesses Achieve Global Success with Bitcoin

While 77 percent of businesses have begun accepting Bitcoin payments because of lower transaction fees (Deloitte Development, 2023), there is also the added benefit of expanding one's customer base to encompass potentially the ends of the world itself. Amongst large e-commerce companies, Overstock.com was a pioneer in accepting Bitcoin (Jones, 2023), extending its market reach to those people TradFi systems had left behind.

On the other side of the world, this move was reciprocated by Kenyan company BitPesa. This allowed them to form new relationships with consumers in Uganda, Congo, and Tanzania, putting them on a more even footing with international economic giants (Jones, 2023).

Research firm Forrester Consulting published a study showing that among businesses that have elected to adopt Bitcoin, *40 percent* of those who utilized the new payment system were *first-time customers* (Jahosky, 2020). Those surveyed in the study saw an average 327 percent return on investment for any money spent setting up crypto payments.

For many consumers, crypto is a way of life: an opportunity to get back at the elite who enriched themselves at the cost of widespread poverty for decades. Therefore engaging in commerce with companies accepting Bitcoin as payment is more than a matter of convenience. It is an inherent duty if one expects to "alter or abolish" the systems that have put us through this "long train of abuses." It is a chance to not just pay smaller transaction fees, but also form relationships with people who support true income equality with their actions, and not just their words, by their adoption of free and fair financial systems.

This demographic of customers will show Bitcoin-accepting businesses a loyalty TradFi institutions could only dream of. "Vote with your dollars," is quickly becoming, "Vote with your Satoshis."

Customers paying in Bitcoin tend to place larger orders. If a person acquires enough Bitcoin to use it as his preferred currency, then he likely has a high degree of financial awareness.

Therefore, it is reasonable to expect this demographic of consumers would be in a better financial situation on average. Perhaps this is why, according to Forrester's study, the average order value for payments made using a cryptocurrency was $157 higher for gift cards, $185 more for electronics, and $3,000 more for precious metals (Forrester Consulting, 2020).

How Bitcoin Boosts Global Remittance to Vulnerable Populations

The 2021 withdrawal of the United States Military from Afghanistan left a vacuum of power to be filled by Taliban forces. Along with the withdrawal came an abrupt end to foreign aid (40 percent of the nation's GDP), and the freezing of $9 billion of central bank assets (Jahani, 2021). Is it any wonder Afghanistan is nearing the top of the list of the Global Crypto Adoption Index (Chainalysis, 2021)?

Remittances reached nearly eight hundred million in Afghanistan amid the nation's new crisis. In other nations, such as Somalia and Tajikistan, remittance makes up more than a quarter of GDP (Keshner, 2021). In other countries where inflation has spiked, Bitcoin remittance payments have spiked along with it, such as Lebanon and Venezuela (Jahani, 2021).

According to CIA figures from before the Afghanistan withdrawal, over 50 percent of the population of Afghanistan lives below the poverty line (Central Intelligence Agency, 2023). Since currencies can have large discrepancies when being converted one for another, even sending just a small fraction of one Bitcoin can keep someone afloat for an entire month.

Consider this story of a man hiring a programmer in India:

I asked him, "Can you port this Hive stuff?" He said he would look into it, and after two days he already had a working beta version that actually looked more like an end product to me! I was so amazed with his skills and devotion, I decided to ask for his BTC address so I could send him some appreciation. After transferring 0.5 BTC, he immediately responded, asking if I lost my mind. It seems I just transferred the equivalent of his monthly salary (Joël Valenzuela, 2016).

According to a Stellar Development Foundation's Cross-Border Remittances Report, nearly two-thirds of all who send money back home from overseas pay a fee; within this group, 40 percent will end up losing 6 percent of the value to fees (PYMNTS, 2021). For people living in poverty who depend on remittance for their vital needs, reducing those fees could mean the difference between life and death.

The World Bank reports a $200 remittance could end up incurring a fee of up to 9.3 percent depending on where it's going and how it is getting there, and these costs pay for KYC processing (Seth, 2021).

Because the Bitcoin protocol is largely self-operating, there isn't a need for much human contact, so when you send money with Bitcoin, you aren't having to share some of the money with TradFi employees to cover their salaries, IRAs, and other benefits.

Migrants working in first-world nations and sending money back to their home countries can account for three times the amount of government-funded foreign aid. Analysts tell us this figure would be much larger if people were not dissuaded by hefty fees (Global Radar, 2017).

As Bitcoin becomes easier to use due to the proliferation of software wallet mobile apps and the rollout of better internet connectivity in developing regions, we will see revenue streams to those in dire straits multiply year after year, thanks to Bitcoin's speedy transactions and low fee requirements.

Mohit Davar, chairman of the International Association of Money Transfer Network, shared his vision of a future where "remittances will be commoditized and become free so nobody makes money on them" (Global Radar, 2017).

CHAPTER 9

What Efforts Are Governments Making to Regulate Bitcoin?

Bitcoin was invented, to some degree, in order to deregulate the financial sector: to make it easier for the poor to have a chance to accrue wealth without being shut down due to unreasonable government mandates. But introducing some level of regulation could help stabilize the volatility of Bitcoin's ever fluctuating value.

Even the thirteen colonies of the New World, who had recently taken up arms to secure their independence from the edicts of King George, ratified the Constitution shortly after. In the two and a half centuries since then, Congress has steadily introduced new legislation as modern ethical crises have presented themselves.

In September of 2022, the International Monetary Fund ("IMF") published a report entitled "Regulating the Crypto Ecosystem." Within the document, they claim due to their widely known volatility and low levels of required disclosure, cryptoassets are vulnerable to misuse. The IMF urges authorities to consider laws and surveillance systems that might be implemented to prevent market exploitation.

Cryptocurrency regulations are currently being debated by senior officials within government agencies, banks, and standard-setting organizations.

In 2018, the Financial Action Task Force (FATF) amended its Anti Money Laundering rules (AML) to include cryptocurrencies and the services built around them. Exchange, transfer, and possession of these assets, as well as participation in financial services related to them, fall under the purview of the FATF guidelines (Bains et al., 2022, pg. 29).

The IMF report details several specific regulation enforcement policy changes across the world. These include the MiCA portion (Markets in Crypto Assets) of the European Union's digital finance strategy, which requires issuers to onshore and requires a lengthy regimen of notification requirements for future white papers and marketing related to cryptocurrencies. Government licensure is also touted as a potential regulation to be implemented in the future, specifically for wallet and exchange providers (Bains et al., 2022, pg. 31, para. 1).

In 2017, Japan amended its financial policy to require "operational risk and cybersecurity management, Know-Your-Customer, internal audits, and minimum capital requirement" from crypto providers (Bains et al., 2022, pg. 31, para. 2). Though many Bitcoin investors are wary of regulations being forced upon a technology designed to be open and self-sustaining, these changes seem like a logical step forward in stabilizing the steep and sudden changes in cryptocurrency market values we have seen thus far.

In February 2018, the Financial Market Supervisory Authority of Switzerland established requirements for the creation of new cryptoassets.

In 2021, it made sweeping changes to civil and financial market laws, to introduce blockchain-based securities and to segregate cryptoassets when their custodians file for bankruptcy (Bains et al., 2022, pg. 31, para. 3).

The Central Bank of Nigeria sent out an official decree in 2018, notifying the public, "Cryptoassets are not legal tender in Nigeria." Three years later, they sent out official letterhead to financial institutions, warning them not to provide services for cryptocurrency providers or transactions (Bains et al., 2022, pg. 32, para. 2).

In July of 2019, the Financial Conduct Authority of the United Kingdom issued its "Final Guidance on Cryptoassets," and began surveying cryptocurrency consumers in an effort to expand the agency's understanding of the market. Three years later, the UK Treasury published an official "roadmap" to crypto regulation (Bains et al., 2022, pg. 31, para. 4).

Why Don't More Governments Adopt Bitcoin?

Due to the offshore operations of many cryptocurrency service providers and the use of VPNs, it can be quite challenging to enforce restrictions on the usage of cryptocurrencies. For government agencies with limited resources, enforcement might be even more challenging. For instance, despite stringent local laws, two million Egyptians are believed to own cryptocurrency (Bains et al., 2022, pg. 32, para. 3).

Writing for the World Trade Organization, Emmanuelle Ganne draws a comparison between the separate worlds of law and computer code. The digitalization of law and the rise of the "code is law" idea was postulated by Lawrence Lessig: i.e., computer code is responsible more and more for human behavior, while governments become vestigial organs and struggle to remain a relevant authority in a technologically evolving world. This is because machines are built to interpret code, not law, whereas humans are built to interpret law over computer code (Ganne, 2018, pg. 103).

Blockchain is not coded to recognize national borders or comply with national laws. This can make regulation, especially enforcement, quite difficult. The hammer then comes down on the middlemen (i.e., the local service providers such as exchanges or wallets). Many of these companies have moved to tax shelters or unregulated jurisdictions, and users are clever enough to access them via VPN. The shutting down or overregulation of centralized exchanges may only serve to push users out into decentralized exchanges, which may carry certain risks they were not previously accustomed to dealing with (Bains et al., 2022, pg. 29 para. 3).

History is certainly at a crossroads. In one potential scenario, the governments of the world could form treaties, and a worldwide cooperative crackdown on cryptocurrency could manifest. Another way it might play out in the favor of crypto enthusiasts is if more governments adopted a "can't beat 'em, join 'em" approach, similar to El Salvador.

Decades from now, reluctance to adopt could see first-world nations losing economic power to once-poorer nations who embraced cryptocurrencies wholeheartedly. Along with such a shake-up of economic ranks around the world, we would certainly see many crypto advocates expatriating to escape regulation.

Whichever scenario plays out, cryptocurrencies are sure to be a major catalyst for new legislative precedents in most countries.

Cryptocurrencies and Illicit Activity

Blockchain technology adds a new dimension to finance. Bitcoin was devised as a way to turn the financial sector on its head. Is it any wonder why governments are having a hard time catching up to it, even ten years since its inception? Its decentralized network of untold thousands or millions of computers can present a challenge for government tracking (Institutional Investor, 2014).

Peer-to-peer technology, while having merit, did open the door for the now 24 percent of all internet traffic made up of unauthorized intellectual property sharing (Go Globe, 2023). In the same way governments have not been able to manage such illegal sharing, they don't seem poised to be able to stop the cryptocurrency revolution either.

Everything that can be used for good can also be turned into evil. Guns can be used to stop crime or commit it. Knives can be used to cut food or commit violence. And, yes, cryptocurrencies can be used to buy forbidden items, just as US dollars can. Blockchain can be used to hide wealth, just as cash can.

Banning all of these things would not guarantee a reduction in crime. Contrarily, it would make new criminals, as millions of people, if not billions, who owned legally acquired items would be made into criminals overnight.

People fear what they don't understand. Since Bitcoin is still an infant next to aged currencies (such as the dollar, yen, or pound), most people still don't know what it is, where it came from, where to get it, or how to use it. To them, Bitcoin can sound like a scary thing, because as Hitchcock taught us: the fear of the unknown is the most powerful fear.

Bitcoin education is, therefore, vital, especially for the up-and-coming generation of young consumers and entrepreneurs. In the next chapter, let's put to bed some of these myths and discover some facts about Bitcoin.

CHAPTER 10

DEBUNKING BITCOIN MYTHS AND MISCONCEPTIONS

Avoiding Crypto Scams

Chainalysis reports that in the year 2020, illicit cryptocurrency transactions had a combined value of over $7 billion; a year later, this value doubled to over $14 billion (Chainalysis, 2023, para. 1). Certainly seems like a bad look for crypto advocates, doesn't it?

But this isn't the whole story. Chainalysis' research also discovered that from 2020 to 2021, cryptocurrency usage volume spiked 561 percent. During this time, the amount of illicit crypto use shrank considerably, from 0.62 percent to 0.15 percent (Chainalysis, 2023, para 2-4).

Mainstream media tends to show their bias against Bitcoin, printing exaggerated headlines about how the world is going to end because of Bitcoin mining, or how blockchain is giving birth to a hidden black market. Most of this illicit crypto value, however, is due to "rug pulls" (Chainalysis, 2023, para. 8).

Rug pulls are when an individual or party sets up what appears to be a legitimate cryptocurrency or exchange, seeks investment, and then takes the money and disappears. Far from a widespread "Silk Road" for human trafficking and murder-for-hire operating in plain sight, the bulk of illicit crypto activity comes in the form of untested cryptocurrency startups hoping to get rich quick.

Heidi the Blockchain Chick from Crypto Tips gives a simple bit of advice to protect against such scams—checking your greed:

> There are a lot of warnings to be had. Do not get greedy. Check your greed at the door. That will help you avoid—I'm going to say—100 percent of the scams here. Most people get blinded by their greed, and they're just happy to throw some money at something that they think is going to be a guarantee, and they get screwed over (Crypto Tips, 2023, 3:23).

Another solution to end these types of scams going forward would be a more thorough implementation of code audits. Open-source code projects have always been a hallmark of the crypto sector. Anything closed source should be treated with an air of caution. Exchanges should require exhaustive code audits before new listings are approved. You can avoid these pitfalls by avoiding altcoins and sticking with the tried and true assets, like Bitcoin.

How Blockchain Prevents Money Laundering

According to UN estimates, criminal activity and money laundering account for less than 5 percent of yearly worldwide GDP. Also, compared to the use of traditional currencies, cryptocurrencies are used in crime far less frequently (Lennon & Danise, 2021).

The Rand Corporation writes: "Contrary to popular belief, 99 percent of cryptocurrency transactions are conducted via centralized exchanges, which are often subject to the same KYC regulations as TradFi institutions" (RAND Corporation, 2020, pg.6).

Cryptocurrency-based money laundering is still quite uncommon when compared to the amounts of cash laundered by conventional means (BAE Systems, 2020, pg.20).

The use of cryptocurrencies for terrorist funding is typically intermittent and less widespread than what had been anticipated when compared to more traditional methods of financing (RAND Corporation, 2020, pg. VII).

Many who are unfamiliar with the field of cryptocurrencies may use the term Bitcoin when they actually are referring to cryptocurrencies in general. This same phenomenon was seen in the 1990s: when, at the height of Nintendo's market dominance, all video games were referred to as "Nintendos" (which their lawyers had the headache of trying to stop, or else risk the trademark being lost due to it becoming generic).

In reality, there exists a subset of cryptocurrencies called *privacy coins*, which hold complete anonymity as their number one priority. These, of course, would be the currencies of choice for criminals, one would imagine; though their slow catch-up to Bitcoin's value has not done anything to entice criminals to adopt them.

Bitcoin was actually built with transparency in mind. This is a concept politicians often seem unaware of. They instead imply, without evidence, blockchain was constructed for nefarious purposes.

Writing for Forbes, Susie Ward states:

Bitcoin's public blockchain ledger ensures a level of transparency that criminals would be foolish to ignore. The ability to trace transactions is a fundamental feature of Bitcoin's design. An example of this occurred with the apprehension of a cyber-crime duo, Heather Morgan and Ilya Lichtenstein, who attempted to launder $4.5 billion worth of stolen Bitcoin. Despite their efforts to obscure the funds through numerous transactions, authorities traced their riches back to the initial scam (Ward, 2023).

Due to Bitcoin's built-in transparency, the Bulgarian government was able to seize over 200,000 Bitcoin from hackers. The value of the confiscated coins eventually accrued to cover about 20 percent of the nation's debt (Coin Insider, 2021).

The United States Internal Revenue Service (IRS) entered into a partnership with Chainalysis in an effort to catch criminals who use blockchain to cover their tracks (Jenkinson, 2023). Since the IRS has been granted access to the private firm's blockchain analysis tools, they have been able to seize $10 billion, which would have otherwise ended up in dark net marketplaces.

What Can Governments Do to Be More Helpful?

In light of all this data, it is clear the issue of Bitcoin is much more nuanced than some uninformed politicians or biased media outlets often let on. It's important we let the data rule the debate and not the charged emotions or baseless accusations that make for catchy headlines.

For example, on January 19, 2021, Janet Yellen, speaking on behalf of the incoming Biden administration, wrongly stated without evidence to the Senate Finance Committee, "I think many (cryptocurrencies) are used, at least in a transaction sense, mainly for illicit financing. And I think we really need to examine ways in which we can curtail their use and make sure that anti-money laundering (sic) doesn't occur through those channels" (Lennon & Danise, 2021, para. 2).

Jake Chervinsky of Compound Labs rebutted this claim, saying he was sad to hear Dr. Yellen maintain the fallacious claim that most cryptocurrency use is related to illicit activities. He believes her false assertion is due to her not giving the issue much attention. He also cautioned that Bitcoin is a tiny worry compared to everything else the Treasury Department had on its plate in 2021, during a pandemic and with a potential recession on the horizon (Lennon & Danise, 2021, para. 6).

Instead of focusing on blockchain in particular, the government could ban the use of other applications created specifically to use cryptocurrencies in a nefarious way: such as "tumblers." These services take the value from one wallet and split it up into several wallets, eventually reuniting the value into a new wallet without any tainted history. The process is usually carried out on the dark web (Elliptic, 2019).

By targeting individuals and services who hold nefarious intentions, governments need not condemn the inventions of Nakamoto, nor the hard work of the engineers who have spent a decade bringing his dream to life. Criminal intent is not evident anywhere in the Bitcoin white paper, nor in any known communications with Satoshi, and so those who hold political power or media leverage should take care to educate themselves on the facts of the matter before casting the revolution in a tainted light.

CHAPTER 11

THE FUTURE OF BITCOIN AND BEYOND

How Embracing Bitcoin Helps You Prepare for the Future

Millennials were slammed by the Great Recession of 2008 at a time when many of them were graduating college, moving out of their parents' homes, or otherwise on the verge of becoming financially independent. Continually trying to catch up to what many of them feel is a rigged economy has taken its toll on them emotionally.

Joining them now is Gen Z, who is experiencing a similar fate as the COVID-19 lockdowns ended many financial opportunities for them. Together, these two generations have found a ray of hope with Bitcoin.

As some of them become old enough to campaign for or even become elected officials themselves, acceptance of Bitcoin is sure to become even more commonplace amongst a willing public tired of suffering whiplash from sudden economic catastrophes.

These younger generations have never seen a time like the 1950s. They have never known the prosperity that made Americana famous the world over. They pay $5 per gallon at the pump, but when they watch movies like *Die Hard*, they see signs for $0.74 per gallon or see old photographs from the 1950s advertising $0.20 per gallon.

These people *know* what inflation looks like. Many of them feel on a deep level their heritage and their destiny has been stolen from them. To them, Bitcoin provides a way out of what many feel is a rigged system.

Since the US dollar is now 99.69 percent digital anyhow (Polumbo, 2021) and is no longer "payable to the bearer on demand" (as Federal Reserve notes used to read before the ending of the gold standard), what have we got to lose? Or at least, this is the mindset of many young people seeking the shortest route to their first taste of financial independence.

But caution must also be applied, and education must come before. Many have lost unimaginable sums of value due to hasty financial decisions. This goes for fiat as well as crypto. But seeing as one is newer than the other and is also more technologically sophisticated, greater care should be applied.

Additionally, any new field attracting large transfers of currency will end up creating swathes of new jobs. Some parents enrolled their children in computer programming or web design classes early on, when it may have seemed like nothing more than an odd hobby. Many of those youth got a great head start on high-paying, competitive job fields.

The world of crypto will also create many new companies and jobs, like Chainalysis' blockchain analysis technology, which was contracted for use by the IRS, as we discussed earlier. In the same way, many youth who were raised in the economic rubble caused by the failures of a system they were too young to understand will grow up to not only embrace Bitcoin, but also improve and help evolve it.

Remember: the Bitcoin Improvement Proposal system exists to implement community-contributed code changes into the future of the Bitcoin protocol. In addition to this opportunity, there always exists the need for more secure wallets, stronger forms of encryption, and more efficient algorithms, especially with quantum computing on the horizon.

How DeFi Can Fix Broken Societies

Speaking at the Capitol Hill Gold Standard Conference in Washington DC in 1983, Ron Paul declared there to be "no greater power" than the power to create money and control the purchasing power of money, claiming, "Throughout history this has proven to be the most sought-after monopolistic power of man" (Paul, 1983).

Do we need money in order to have government? Do we need government in order to have money? Are these two things inseparable?

As time races forward and multiple technological advancements multiply each other's effects, who can tell what foreign type of world our children may one day inherit? As Thomas Gresham said in the 1500s, "Good and bad coin cannot circulate together." Will the proliferation of blockchain cause the extinction of fiat currency systems and the wealth inequality they have caused?

Adam Curtis documents in his film *HyperNormalisation* a time in 1970s when the city of New York was unable to pay its debt to the banks, due to exponentially growing welfare obligations and a fleeing tax base:

What happened that day in New York marked a radical shift in power. The banks insisted that in order to protect their loans, they should be allowed to take control of the city. The city appealed to the president, but he refused to help. So a new committee was set up to manage the city's finances. Out of nine members, eight of them were bankers. It was the start of an extraordinary experiment, where the financial institutions took power away from the politicians and started to run society themselves (Curtis, 2016, 5:12).

The borrower is a servant to the lender. How long should we let a small subset of humanity buy up millions of acres of land and concentrate wealth with themselves? Perhaps Jefferson's call to "alter or abolish" is needed now more than ever. Perhaps we need to declare our own independence from failed monetary policies causing widespread poverty throughout the world. Perhaps decentralized finance could grant more freedom to man than the Constitution of the United States ever claimed to.

Currencies not tied to precious metals are like tickets from a carnival game or arcade, to be exchanged for a stuffed animal or similar prize. They have no value themselves, but only serve as a claim check and proof of work performed. But when a tiny fraction of the most powerful have the ability to create the tickets whenever they see fit, without doing said work, and to dole it out to their buddies while others suffer, there is a clearly defined flaw in the system: an injustice which Bitcoin's infallible scarcity can easily remedy.

Bitcoin becoming a widespread store of value might prove to be a civilization-saving event. Developed civilizations need a reliable store of value to build and preserve wealth. When we don't build up savings and instead spend everything we earn (and more, via debt), our infrastructure becomes fragile, societal values become corrupt, and the future becomes highly discounted. We see where this leads to through many historical examples: coin debasements of Ancient Rome led to the empire's collapse; hyperinflations of the twentieth and twenty-first century led to war, totalitarianism, and famine. We can escape this fate, both on the individual and societal level, by embracing Bitcoin" (Tĕtek, 2022).

Anticipating the Future of Bitcoin

What exciting new developments can we expect to see in the future of Bitcoin? The world is at a crossroads in the form of fiery debates centered around cryptocurrency regulations. In addition to this, we will surely see new industries adopting blockchain technology, including social media companies and other industries we may not have considered previously. When the dust settles, we will surely be left with a much more secure digital world, online and offline, thanks to Nakamoto and his team.

Alex Gladstein, chief strategy officer of the Human Rights Foundation, after attending a Bitcoin conference in Africa, recalled how the sheer number of entrepreneurs and significant personalities in the Bitcoin industry, hailing from so many different countries, shocked him. He said he believes the most important news item for the coming years will certainly be worldwide Bitcoin adoption (Wilser & Luo, 2022).

Writing for Market Business News, David Jones reasoned that the importance of Bitcoin to the global economy will be carefully debated by experts for years to come (Jones, 2023).

Bill Barhydt of CoinDesk weighs in on Bitcoin's impact, saying it is creating its own economy independent of anything coming before it and is not a mere update of an existing economy (Barhydt, 2018).

The consequences of Bitcoin are not yet fully realized, as humanity has never previously experienced a currency with an immutable issuance timeline and unchangeable number of units (Frontier Bank, 2022).

Cointelegraph speculated: if the government's most crucial task is the protection of private property, then blockchain may be the last frontier and in many ways replace the need for governments. Over the next fifty years, it may render reliance on centralized state governments outdated and unneeded (Joël Valenzuela, 2016).

Susie Ward of *Forbes* urges us to accept the greater utility of Bitcoin, in order to unlock its full transformative potential for financial institutions and usher in a new era of economic opportunity and financial purity (Ward, 2023).

Bitcoin is much more heavily adopted in regions where the alternative is unviable. If governments want to crack down on a competing system but have failed to uphold one which benefits the people, then many people will simply find a way to circumvent restrictions, feeling they have run out of options to provide for themselves and their loved ones.

Instead of responding with violence or sanctions, perhaps governments should focus their enforcement powers inwardly: assessing what has drawn their people away to another financial system, and implementing changes to their own in order to remain competitive.

Bitcoin Magazine analyst Rachita Nayar warns of the consequences of future government interference in the adoption of Bitcoin. In her mind, Bitcoin technology would continue to exist even if the federal government sought to criminalize it, foreign markets and investors would thrive on it, and overregulated jurisdictions would fall behind economically. She warns us: killing off innovation cannot benefit a society. Additionally, she advocates for cryptocurrency proficiency education for youth, seeing as blockchain technology will endure for a very long time (Nayar, 2021, para. 11).

> Bans on Bitcoin are harmful to the economy and disregard individual Americans' rights to manage their own money as they see appropriate. These calls also fail to address the underlying issue: over half of all Americans live paycheck to paycheck. The government must fulfill its duty to provide every child with an education for financial responsibility. Tens of millions of ordinary Americans have invested in Bitcoin as a means of accumulating real wealth. It is difficult enough for ordinary individuals to advance. It is inconceivable to believe that the government could adopt a law that would destroy all of those gains with the stroke of a pen (Nayar, 2021, para. 12).

Going forward, we will also see the shift from Web 2.0 to Web 3.0: the next phase of the evolution of the internet. We will see users taking control of their data back from companies who profit from it.

This will be a less centralized internet, incorporating more of the technology Adam Back and Satoshi pioneered in the 1990s and early 2000s.

Since this new internet will be governed less by human intelligence and more by smart contracts and artificial intelligence, engineers will have to work tirelessly to ensure robust security, because open-source code will become the norm, and blockchain implementation will set new standards in transparency. Banning the technology, which may very well end up being the foundation of all digital systems going forward, would be like the civilizations that came before us had banning the wheel or the combustion engine.

In a democratic election, the losing contender is expected to concede when the results are fairly counted. Those who have been given the power to print paper money may have to one day concede that their system, which contributed to the financial ruin of countless lives, has lost the hearts of the people who favor one better suited to their needs.

But what will the future of Bitcoin hold for *you*? If you expect to live for thirty years after retirement, based on the current average cost of living in the United States ($5,000 a month for a 2.5 person household), you will need $1.3 million. To add the recommended 15 percent cushion for unforeseen expenses, we'll round the figure up to $1.5 million (Farfan, 2023).

Based on 2030 Bitcoin price projections by industry experts ranging from $100,000 (CryptoGlobe, 2022) to $400,000 (Bloomberg, 2021) to $12 million (Finbold, 2022), you would need 14.74 BTC, 3.74 BTC, and 0.12 BTC, respectively, to retire on

Bitcoin in 2030 (Farfan, 2023). Retirement providers such as Fidelity are now offering Bitcoin options with their 401(k) plans, so it's easier than ever before.

The best time to invest in Bitcoin is always right now. Hopefully the information in this book has given you a place to start in your understanding of what Bitcoin can mean for our society and the world as we move toward an uncertain future. Whether you agree on Bitcoin's transformational potential or not, there's no arguing it's here to stay. While I don't recommend putting your entire worth into Bitcoin, it's certainly reasonable to place a percentage of your hard-earned wealth into this exciting new store of value. I have.

BITCOIN: A PEER-TO-PEER ELECTRONIC CASH SYSTEM

SATOSHI NAKAMOTO

OCTOBER 31, 2008

Abstract

A purely peer-to-peer version of electronic cash would allow online payments to be sent directly from one party to another without going through a financial institution. Digital signatures provide part of the solution, but the main benefits are lost if a trusted third party is still required to prevent double-spending. We propose a solution to the double-spending problem using a peer-to-peer network. The network timestamps transactions by hashing them into an ongoing chain of hash-based proof-of-work, forming a record that cannot be changed without redoing the proof-of-work. The longest chain not only serves as proof of the sequence of events witnessed, but proof that it came from the largest pool of CPU power. As long as a majority of CPU power is controlled by nodes that are not cooperating to attack the network, they'll generate the longest chain and outpace attackers. The network itself requires minimal structure. Messages are broadcast on a best-effort basis, and nodes can leave and rejoin the network at will, accepting the longest proof-of-work chain as proof of what happened while they were gone.

1. Introduction

Commerce on the internet has come to rely almost exclusively on financial institutions serving as trusted third parties to process electronic payments. While the system works well enough for most transactions, it still suffers from the inherent weaknesses of the trust-based model. Completely non-reversible transactions are not really possible, since financial institutions cannot avoid mediating disputes. The cost of mediation increases transaction costs, limiting the minimum practical transaction size and cutting off the possibility for small casual transactions, and there is a broader cost in the loss of ability to make non-reversible payments for non-reversible services. With the possibility of reversal, the need for trust spreads. Merchants must be wary of their customers, hassling them for more information than they would otherwise need. A certain percentage of fraud is accepted as unavoidable. These costs and payment uncertainties can be avoided in person by using physical currency, but no mechanism exists to make payments over a communications channel without a trusted party.

What is needed is an electronic payment system based on cryptographic proof instead of trust, allowing any two willing parties to transact directly with each other without the need for a trusted third party. Transactions that are computationally impractical to reverse would protect sellers from fraud, and routine escrow mechanisms could easily be implemented to protect buyers. In this paper, we propose a solution to the double-spending problem using a peer-to-peer distributed timestamp server to generate computational proof of the chronological order of transactions.

The system is secure as long as honest nodes collectively control more CPU power than any cooperating group of attacker nodes.

2. Transactions

We define an electronic coin as a chain of digital signatures. Each owner transfers the coin to the next by digitally signing a hash of the previous transaction and the public key of the next owner and adding these to the end of the coin. A payee can verify the signatures to verify the chain of ownership.

The problem, of course, is the payee can't verify that one of the owners did not double-spend the coin. A common solution is to introduce a trusted central authority, or *mint,* that checks every transaction for double-spending. After each transaction, the coin must be returned to the mint to issue a new coin, and only coins issued directly from the mint are trusted not to be double-spent. The problem with this solution is that the fate of the entire money system depends on the company running the mint, with every transaction having to go through them, just like a bank.

We need a way for the payee to know that the previous owners did not sign any earlier transactions. For our purposes, the earliest transaction is the one that counts, so we don't care about later attempts to double-spend. The only way to confirm the absence of a transaction is to be aware of all transactions. In the mint-based model, the mint was aware of all transactions and decided which arrived first. To accomplish this without a trusted party, transactions must be publicly announced,[1] and we need a system for participants to agree on a single history of the order in which they were received.

The payee needs proof that at the time of each transaction, the majority of nodes agreed it was the first received.

3. Timestamp Server

The solution we propose begins with a timestamp server. A *timestamp server* works by taking a hash of a block of items to be timestamped and widely publishing the hash, such as in a newspaper or Usenet post.[2-5] The timestamp proves that the data must have existed at the time, obviously, in order to get into the hash. Each timestamp includes the previous timestamp in its hash, forming a chain, with each additional timestamp reinforcing the ones before it.

4. Proof-of-Work

To implement a distributed timestamp server on a peer-to-peer basis, we will need to use a proof-of-work system similar to Adam Back's Hashcash,[6] rather than newspaper or Usenet posts. The proof-of-work involves scanning for a value that, when hashed, such as with SHA-256, the hash begins with a number of zero bits. The average work required is exponential in the number of zero bits required and can be verified by executing a single hash.

For our timestamp network, we implement the proof-of-work by incrementing a nonce in the block until a value is found that gives the block's hash the required zero bits. Once the CPU effort has been expended to make it satisfy the proof-of-work, the block cannot be changed without redoing the work. As later blocks are chained after it, the work to change the block would include redoing all the blocks after it.

The proof-of-work also solves the problem of determining representation in majority decision-making. If the majority were based on "one IP address, one vote," it could be subverted by anyone able to allocate many IPs. Proof-of-work is essentially one CPU, one vote. The majority decision is represented by the longest chain, which has the greatest proof-of-work effort invested in it. If a majority of CPU power is controlled by honest nodes, the honest chain will grow the fastest and outpace any competing chains. To modify a past block, an attacker would have to redo the proof-of-work of the block and all blocks after it and then catch up with and surpass the work of the honest nodes. We will show later that the probability of a slower attacker catching up diminishes exponentially as subsequent blocks are added.

To compensate for increasing hardware speed and varying interest in running nodes over time, the proof-of-work difficulty is determined by a moving average targeting an average number of blocks per hour. If they're generated too fast, the difficulty increases.

5. Network

The steps to run the network are as follows:

1. New transactions are broadcast to all nodes.
2. Each node collects new transactions into a block.
3. Each node works on finding a difficult proof-of-work for its block.
4. When a node finds a proof-of-work, it broadcasts the block to all nodes.

5. Nodes accept the block only if all transactions in it are valid and not already spent.

6. Nodes express their acceptance of the block by working on creating the next block in the chain, using the hash of the accepted block as the previous hash.

Nodes always consider the longest chain to be the correct one and will keep working on extending it. If two nodes broadcast different versions of the next block simultaneously, some nodes may receive one or the other first. In that case, they work on the first one they received but save the other branch in case it becomes longer. The tie will be broken when the next proof-of-work is found and one branch becomes longer; the nodes that were working on the other branch will then switch to the longer one.

New transaction broadcasts do not necessarily need to reach all nodes. As long as they reach many nodes, they will get into a block before long. Block broadcasts are also tolerant of dropped messages. If a node does not receive a block, it will request it when it receives the next block and realizes it missed one.

6. Incentive

By convention, the first transaction in a block is a special transaction that starts a new coin owned by the creator of the block. This adds an incentive for nodes to support the network and provides a way to initially distribute coins into circulation, since there is no central authority to issue them.

The steady addition of a constant amount of new coins is analogous to gold miners expending resources to add gold to circulation. In our case, it is CPU time and electricity that is expended.

The incentive can also be funded with transaction fees. If the output value of a transaction is less than its input value, the difference is a transaction fee that is added to the incentive value of the block containing the transaction. Once a predetermined number of coins have entered circulation, the incentive can transition entirely to transaction fees and be completely inflation-free.

The incentive may help encourage nodes to stay honest. If a greedy attacker is able to assemble more CPU power than all the honest nodes, he would have to choose between using it to defraud people by stealing back his payments or using it to generate new coins. He ought to find it more profitable to play by the rules, such rules that favour him with more new coins than everyone else combined, than to undermine the system and the validity of his own wealth.

7. Reclaiming Disk Space

Once the latest transaction in a coin is buried under enough blocks, the spent transactions before it can be discarded to save disk space. To facilitate this without breaking the block's hash, transactions are hashed in a Merkle Tree,[7][2][5] with only the root included in the block's hash. Old blocks can then be compacted by stubbing off branches of the tree. The interior hashes do not need to be stored.

A block header with no transactions would be about 80 bytes. If we suppose blocks are generated every ten minutes, 80 bytes * 6 * 24 * 365 = 4.2MB per year. With computer systems typically selling with 2GB of RAM as of 2008, and Moore's Law predicting current growth of 1.2GB per year, storage should not be a problem even if the block headers must be kept in memory.

8. Simplified Payment Verification

It is possible to verify payments without running a full network node. A user only needs to keep a copy of the block headers of the longest proof-of-work chain, which he can get by querying network nodes until he's convinced he has the longest chain, and obtain the Merkle branch linking the transaction to the block it's timestamped in. He can't check the transaction for himself, but by linking it to a place in the chain, he can see that a network node has accepted it, and blocks added after it further confirm the network has accepted it.

As such, the verification is reliable as long as honest nodes control the network, but is more vulnerable if the network is overpowered by an attacker. While network nodes can verify transactions for themselves, the simplified method can be fooled by an attacker's fabricated transactions for as long as the attacker can continue to overpower the network. One strategy to protect against this would be to accept alerts from network nodes when they detect an invalid block, prompting the user's software to download the full block and alerted transactions to confirm the inconsistency.

Businesses that receive frequent payments will probably still want to run their own nodes for more independent security and quicker verification.

9. Combining and Splitting Value

Although it would be possible to handle coins individually, it would be unwieldy to make a separate transaction for every cent in a transfer. To allow value to be split and combined, transactions contain multiple inputs and outputs. Normally there will be either a single input from a larger previous transaction or multiple inputs combining smaller amounts, and at most two outputs: one for the payment and one returning the change, if any, back to the sender.

It should be noted that fan-out, where a transaction depends on several transactions, and those transactions depend on many more, is not a problem here. There is never the need to extract a complete standalone copy of a transaction's history.

10. Privacy

The traditional banking model achieves a level of privacy by limiting access to information to the parties involved and the trusted third party. The necessity to announce all transactions publicly precludes this method, but privacy can still be maintained by breaking the flow of information in another place: by keeping public keys anonymous. The public can see that someone is sending an amount to someone else, but without information linking the transaction to anyone.

This is similar to the level of information released by stock exchanges, where the time and size of individual trades, the "tape," is made public, but without telling who the parties were.

As an additional firewall, a new key pair should be used for each transaction to keep them from being linked to a common owner. Some linking is still unavoidable with multi-input transactions, which necessarily reveal that their inputs were owned by the same owner. The risk is that if the owner of a key is revealed, linking could reveal other transactions that belonged to the same owner.

11. Calculations

We consider the scenario of an attacker trying to generate an alternate chain faster than the honest chain. Even if this is accomplished, it does not throw the system open to arbitrary changes, such as creating value out of thin air or taking money that never belonged to the attacker. Nodes are not going to accept an invalid transaction as payment, and honest nodes will never accept a block containing them. An attacker can only try to change one of his own transactions to take back money he recently spent.

The race between the honest chain and an attacker chain can be characterized as a Binomial Random Walk. The success event is the honest chain being extended by one block, increasing its lead by +1, and the failure event is the attacker's chain being extended by one block, reducing the gap by -1.

The probability of an attacker catching up from a given deficit is analogous to a Gambler's Ruin problem.

Suppose a gambler with unlimited credit starts at a deficit and plays potentially an infinite number of trials to try to reach breakeven. We can calculate the probability he ever reaches breakeven, or that an attacker ever catches up with the honest chain, as follows:[8]

p = probability an honest node finds the next block

q = probability the attacker finds the next block

q_z = probability the attacker will ever catch up from z blocks behind

Given our assumption that $p>q$, the probability drops exponentially as the number of blocks the attacker has to catch up with increases. With the odds against him, if he doesn't make a lucky lunge forward early on, his chances become vanishingly small as he falls further behind.

We now consider how long the recipient of a new transaction needs to wait before being sufficiently certain the sender can't change the transaction. We assume the sender is an attacker who wants to make the recipient believe he paid him for a while, then switch it to pay back to himself after some time has passed. The receiver will be alerted when that happens, but the sender hopes it will be too late.

The receiver generates a new key pair and gives the public key to the sender shortly before signing. This prevents the sender from preparing a chain of blocks ahead of time by working on it continuously until he is lucky enough to get far enough ahead, then executing the transaction at that moment. Once the transaction is sent, the dishonest sender starts working in secret on a parallel chain containing an alternate version of his transaction.

The recipient waits until the transaction has been added to a block and z blocks have been linked after it. He doesn't know the exact amount of progress the attacker has made, but assuming the honest blocks took the average expected time per block, the attacker's potential progress will be a Poisson distribution with expected value:

$$\lambda = z(q/p)$$

To get the probability the attacker could still catch up now, we multiply the Poisson density for each amount of progress he could have made by the probability he could catch up from that point:

$$\sum_{k=0}^{\infty} \frac{\lambda^k e^{-\lambda}}{k!} \cdot \{ (q/p)^{(z-k)} \; 1 \; if \; k \le z \; if \; k > z \}$$

Rearranging to avoid summing the infinite tail of the distribution . . .

$$1 - \sum_{k=0}^{z} \frac{\lambda^k e^{-\lambda}}{k!} (1 - (q/p)^{(z-k)})$$

Converting to C code . . .

```
#include

double AttackerSuccessProbability(double q, int z)

{

double p = 1.0 - q;

double lambda = z * (q / p);

double sum = 1.0;

int i, k;

for (k = 0; k <= z; k++)

{
```

```
double poisson = exp(-lambda);

for (i = 1; i <= k; i++)

poisson *= lambda / i;

sum -= poisson * (1 - pow(q / p, z - k));

}

return sum;

}
```

Running some results, we can see the probability drop off exponentially with z

q=0.1

z=0 P=1.0000000

z=1 P=0.2045873

z=2 P=0.0509779

z=3 P=0.0131722

z=4 P=0.0034552

z=5 P=0.0009137

z=6 P=0.0002428

z=7 P=0.0000647

z=8 P=0.0000173

z=9 P=0.0000046

z=10 P=0.0000012

q=0.3

z=0 P=1.0000000

z=5 P=0.1773523

z=10 P=0.0416605

z=15 P=0.0101008

z=20 P=0.0024804

z=25 P=0.0006132

z=30 P=0.0001522

z=35 P=0.0000379

z=40 P=0.0000095

z=45 P=0.0000024

z=50 P=0.0000006

Solving for P less than 0.1 percent...

P < 0.001

q=0.10 z=5

q=0.15 z=8

q=0.20 z=11

q=0.25 z=15

q=0.30 z=24

q=0.35 z=41

q=0.40 z=89

q=0.45 z=340

12. Conclusion

We have proposed a system for electronic transactions without relying on trust. We started with the usual framework of coins made from digital signatures, which provides strong control of ownership, but is incomplete without a way to prevent double-spending. To solve this, we proposed a peer-to-peer network using proof-of-work to record a public history of transactions that quickly becomes computationally impractical for an attacker to change if honest nodes control a majority of CPU power. The network is robust in its unstructured simplicity. Nodes work all at once with little coordination. They do not need to be identified, since messages are not routed to any particular place and only need to be delivered on a best-effort basis. Nodes can leave and rejoin the network at will, accepting the proof-of-work chain as proof of what happened while they were gone. They vote with their CPU power, expressing their acceptance of valid blocks by working on extending them and rejecting invalid blocks by refusing to work on them. Any needed rules and incentives can be enforced with this consensus mechanism.

References

1. W. Dai, "b-money," http://www.weidai.com/bmoney.txt, 1998. ↩

2. H. Massias, X.S. Avila, and J.-J. Quisquater, "Design of a secure timestamping service with minimal trust requirements," In *20th Symposium on Information Theory in the Benelux*, May 1999. ↩ ↩

3. S. Haber, W.S. Stornetta, "How to time-stamp a digital document," In *Journal of Cryptology*, vol 3, no 2, pages 99-111, 1991. ↩

4. D. Bayer, S. Haber, W.S. Stornetta, "Improving the efficiency and reliability of digital time-stamping," In *Sequences II: Methods in Communication, Security and Computer Science*, pages 329-334, 1993. ↩

5. S. Haber, W.S. Stornetta, "Secure names for bit-strings," In *Proceedings of the 4th ACM Conference on Computer and Communications Security*, pages 28-35, April 1997. ↵ ↵

6. A. Back, "Hashcash - a denial of service counter-measure," http://www.hashcash.org/papers/hashcash.pdf, 2002. ↵

7. R.C. Merkle, "Protocols for public key cryptosystems," In *Proc. 1980 Symposium on Security and Privacy*, IEEE Computer Society, pages 122-133, April 1980. ↵

8. W. Feller, "An introduction to probability theory and its applications," 1957. ↵

REFERENCES

ABECOIN. (2022, December 10). *If Exodus, Ledger, Trezor or Trust go Bust, Do THIS!* YouTube. Retrieved August 15, 2023, from https://www.youtube.com/watch?v=uN4N6Rni6dc.

Acemoglu, D., Acemoglu, D., & Robinson, J. A. (2013). Why Nations Fail: The Origins of Power, Prosperity, and Poverty. Crown.

Acohido, B. (2009, January 20). "Hackers Breach Heartland Payment Credit Card System." ABC News. Retrieved August 2, 2023, from https://abcnews.go.com/Business/PersonalFinance/story?id=6695611&page=1.

Akashmomale. (2022, August 30). "Bitcoin vs. Dogecoin—7 Differences Between Bitcoin and Dogecoin." GeeksforGeeks. Retrieved August 10, 2023, from https://www.geeksforgeeks.org/bitcoin-vs-dogecoin-7-differences-between-bitcoin-and-dogecoin/#.

Ali, A. (2021, April 12). *"Bitcoin Is the Fastest Asset to Reach a $1 Trillion Market Cap."* Visual Capitalist. Retrieved August 4, 2023, from https://www.visualcapitalist.com/bitcoin-is-the-fastest-asset-to-reach-a-1-trillion-market-cap/.

Altraide, D. (2022, October 28). "How the 2008 Financial Crisis Still Affects You." YouTube. Retrieved July 26, 2023, from https://www.youtube.com/watch?v=U1dpWiZoiJU.

Andresen, G. (2010, June 12). "Get 5 Free Bitcoins from Freebitcoins.Appspot.Com." Bitcoin Forum. Retrieved August 5, 2023, from https://bitcointalk.org/index.php?topic=183.0.

Andresen, G. (2010, November 3). "Bitcoin Is Not as Advertised." Bitcoin Forum. Retrieved July 30, 2023, from https://bitcointalk.org/index.php?topic=1647.60.

Andrews, E. (2016, February 17). "What Was the Sword of Damocles?" Retrieved July 25, 2023, from https://www.history.com/news/what-was-the-sword-of-damocles.

Apple Inc. (2021, February 18). "Security of Runtime Process in iOS and iPadOS." Apple Support. Retrieved August 15, 2023, from https://support.apple.com/guide/security/security-of-runtime-process-sec15bfe098e/web.

Ashmore, D. (2023, February 21). "What Is Ethereum Classic?" Forbes Advisor. Forbes.com. Retrieved August 14, 2023, from https://www.forbes.com/advisor/investing/cryptocurrency/what-is-ethereum-classic/.

BAE Systems. (2020, February 2). "Follow the Money." Swift. Retrieved August 21, 2023, from https://www.swift.com/sites/default/files/files/swift_bae_report_Follow-The percent20Money.pdf.

Bains, P., Ismail, A., & Melo, F. (2022, September). "Regulating the Crypto Ecosystem: The Case of Unbacked Crypto Assets." International Monetary Fund. Retrieved August 19, 2023, from https://www.imf.org/-/media/Files/Publications/FTN063/2022/English/FTNEA2022007.ashx/

Barhydt, B. (2018, October 27). "The Double-Spend (What Bitcoin's White Paper Solved Forever)." CoinDesk. Retrieved August 1, 2023, from https://www.coindesk.com/markets/2018/10/27/the-double-spend-what-bitcoins-white-paper-solved-forever/.

BBC. (2017, March 3). "Bitcoin Value Tops Gold for First Time." BBC. Retrieved August 5, 2023, from https://www.bbc.com/news/business-39149475.

BBC. (2017, September 8). "Massive Equifax Data Breach Hits 143 Million." BBC. Retrieved August 2, 2023, from https://www.bbc.com/news/business-41192163.

Ben-Naim, A. (2019, November 29). "Entropy and Information Theory: Uses and Misuses - PMC." NCBI. Retrieved August 3, 2023, from https://www.ncbi.nlm.nih.gov/pmc/articles/PMC7514515/.

Bitcoin.com. (2022, March 18). "What Is a DEX?" Bitcoin.com. Retrieved August 15, 2023, from https://www.bitcoin.com/get-started/what-is-a-dex/.

Bitcoin.it. (2022, April 8). "Hashcash." Bitcoin Wiki. Retrieved August 9, 2023, from https://en.bitcoin.it/wiki/Hashcash.

Bitcoin Project. (2013, October 2). "Protect Your Privacy." Bitcoin.org. Retrieved August 2, 2023, from https://bitcoin.org/en/protect-your-privacy.

Bitcoin Wiki. (2019, April 24). "Secp256k1." Bitcoin Wiki. Retrieved August 16, 2023, from https://en.bitcoin.it/wiki/Secp256k1.

Blockchain Media Group. (2019, October 30). "Satoshi's Final Messages Leave Tantalizing Clues to His Disappearance." The Bitcoin News. Retrieved July 30, 2023, from https://thebitcoinnews.com/satoshis-final-messages-leave-tantalizing-clues-to-his-disappearance/.

Blockchair. (2023, August 5). "Bitcoin / Address / 1A1zP1eP5QGefi2DMPTfTL5SLmv7DivfNa." Blockchair. Retrieved August 5, 2023, from https://blockchair.com/bitcoin/address/1A1zP1eP5QGefi2DMPTfTL5SLmv7DivfNa.

Bloomberg. (2021, April 1). "Rising Bitcoin Adoption Tide." Bloomberg Professional Services. Retrieved August 22, 2023, from https://assets.bbhub.io/promo/sites/12/1060725_Crypto-Apr2021Outlook.pdf?utm_source=Email&utm_campaign=Indices&utm_medium=Newsletter&utm_content=CryptoOutlook-Apr2021&tactic=475077&link=button-bottom.

Blount, J. (2019, September 5). "These Startups Show Blockchain's Potential in Various Industries." Forbes. Retrieved August 3, 2023, from https://www.forbes.com/sites/joresablount/2019/09/05/these-startups-show-blockchains-potential-in-various-industries/?sh=30a67ede6e0b.

Book, J. (2023, June 14). "What Is Hyperinflation and How Does It Happen?" Bitcoin Magazine. Retrieved August 4, 2023, from https://bitcoinmagazine.com/guides/what-is-hyperinflation.

Browne, R. (2022, May 18). "China Is Second-Biggest Bitcoin Mining Hub Despite Beijing's Ban." CNBC. Retrieved August 1, 2023, from https://www.cnbc.com/2022/05/18/china-is-second-biggest-bitcoin-mining-hub-as-miners-go-underground.html.

Brunell, N. (2023, June 13). "$1 TRILLION Dollar Birthday Present." Rumble. Retrieved August 4, 2023, from https://rumble.com/vywmi5-1-trillion-dollar-birthday-present.html.

Business Insider. (2017, September 23). "Lending App MicroMoney to Raise $30Mln Through an ICO in October, Helping Bring 2 Bln Unbanked Into the New Crypto-Economy." Markets Insider. Retrieved August 2, 2023, from https://markets.businessinsider.com/news/stocks/lending-app-micromoney-to-raise-$30mln-through-an-ico-in-october-helping-bring-2-bln-unbanked-into-the-new-crypto-economy-707226.

Canadian Bitcoiners Podcast. (2023, January 8). Twitter. Retrieved August 24, 2023, from https://twitter.com/PraveenPerera/status/1612470866171891712.

Central Intelligence Agency. (2023, August 15). "Photos of Afghanistan - The World Factbook." CIA. Retrieved August 18, 2023, from https://www.cia.gov/the-world-factbook/countries/afghanistan/#economy.

Chainalysis. (2021, October 14). "Global Crypto Adoption Up 880 percent in 2021 - Chainalysis." Chainalysis Blog. Retrieved August 18, 2023, from https://blog.chainalysis.com/reports/2021-global-crypto-adoption-index/.

Chainalysis. (2023, January 12). "2023 Crypto Crime Trends: Illicit Cryptocurrency Volumes Reach All-Time Highs Amid Surge in Sanctions Designations and Hacking." Chainalysis. Retrieved August 21, 2023, from https://www.chainalysis.com/blog/2022-crypto-crime-report-introduction/.

Cheong, W. (2019, December 20). "This Is How Bitcoin Can Help End Income Inequality in 2020." Business Insider. Retrieved August 2, 2023, from https://www.businessinsider.com/this-is-how-bitcoin-can-end-income-inequality-in-2020.

CNBC. (2017, October 27). "Mystery Founder Of Bitcoin: Uncovering Satoshi Nakamoto's Identity Of Bitcoin Matters | CNBC." YouTube. Retrieved July 30, 2023, from https://www.youtube.com/watch?v=Bze53qwHS8o.

Coinbase. (2023, July 29). "Bitcoin (BTC) Price, Charts, and News. Coinbase." Retrieved July 29, 2023, from https://www.coinbase.com/price/bitcoin.

Coin Guides. (2019, May 9). "What Is Bitcoin Reorg? Is It Really Possible to Reorg Bitcoin Blockchain?" Coin Guides. Retrieved August 3, 2023, from https://coinguides.org/bitcoin-reorg-explained/.

Coin Guides. (2021, July 12). "Bitcoin Confirmations - All You Need to Know about Block Confirmations." Coin Guides. Retrieved August 3, 2023, from https://coinguides.org/confirmations/.

Coin Insider. (2021, July 9). "Bulgarian Government Actually Owns $3 Billion USD in Bitcoin." Coin Insider. Retrieved August 21, 2023, from https://www.coininsider.com/bulgarian-government-owns-3-billion-usd-bitcoin/.

Cointree. (2021, September 21). "Cryptocurrency vs. Stock Market: What's the Difference?" Cointree. Retrieved August 14, 2023, from https://www.cointree.com/learn/cryptocurrency-exchange-vs-stock-exchange/.

Competiello, C. (2019, December 11). "Bitcoin Price Could Hit $500,000 in 10 Years, Better Than Gold: Yusko." Business Insider. Retrieved August 2, 2023, from https://www.businessinsider.com/bitcoin-price-could-hit-500000-10-years-gold-mark-yusko-2019-12.

Corbett, J. (Director). (2014). *Century of Enslavement: The History of the Federal Reserve* [Film]. https://www.imdb.com/title/tt6002200/.

Cornell Law School. (2021, December 3)." Coinage Power | U.S. Constitution Annotated | US Law | LII / Legal Information Institute." Law.Cornell.Edu. Retrieved July 26, 2023, from https://www.law.cornell.edu/constitution-conan/article-1/section-8/clause-5/coinage-power.

CryptoGlobe. (2022, September 21). "Bitcoin ($BTC) Price Hitting $100000 Is a 'Matter of Time,' Says Bloomberg Analyst." CryptoGlobe. Retrieved August 22, 2023, from https://www.cryptoglobe.com/latest/2022/09/bitcoin-btc-price-hitting-100000-is-a-matter-of-time-says-bloomberg-analyst/.

Crypto Tips. (2022, December 22). "Which Mobile Wallets Are Actually Secure?" [FULL INTERVIEW]. YouTube. Retrieved August 14, 2023, from https://www.youtube.com/watch?v=cSCtlKsW4Zo.

Crypto Tips. (2023, August 21). "New Crypto Scams Are HERE." YouTube. Retrieved August 21, 2023, from https://www.youtube.com/watch?v=UkwqZVK3_QA.

Crypto Tips. (2023, August 22). "There's a Bull Market in Crypto RIGHT NOW! Are You Missing It?" YouTube. Retrieved August 22, 2023, from https://www.youtube.com/watch?v=6Ldhg-dcoFw.

Curtis, A. (Director). (2016). *HyperNormalisation* [Film]. https://www.bbc.co.uk/iplayer/episode/p04b183c/hypernormalisation.

De Chant, T. (2021, May 6). "China's Carbon Pollution Now Surpasses All Developed Countries Combined." Ars Technica. Retrieved August 1, 2023, from https://arstechnica.com/tech-policy/2021/05/chinas-carbon-pollution-now-surpasses-all-developed-countries-combined/.

Dehner, C. (2009, June 16). "Hyperinflation: The Story of 9 Failed Currencies." Mint. Retrieved July 26, 2023, from https://mint.intuit.com/blog/trends/hyperinflation-the-story-of-9-failed-currencies/.

Deloitte Development. (2023, June). "Cryptocurrency Benefits for Corporations." Deloitte. Retrieved August 18, 2023, from https://www2.deloitte.com/us/en/pages/audit/articles/corporates-using-crypto.html.

Deloitte Insights. (2019, May 3). "Deloitte's 2019 Global Blockchain Survey." Deloitte. Retrieved August 3, 2023, from https://www2.deloitte.com/content/dam/Deloitte/se/Documents/risk/DI_2019-global-blockchain-survey.pdf.

Desjardins, J., & Rao, P. (2014, July 9). "How Bitcoin Can and Will Disrupt the Financial System." Visual Capitalist. Retrieved August 17, 2023, from https://www.visualcapitalist.com/how-bitcoin-can-and-will-disrupt-financial-system/.

Duignan, B. (2023, June 23). "Great Recession | Causes, Effects, Statistics, & Facts." Britannica. Retrieved July 26, 2023, from https://www.britannica.com/money/topic/great-recession.

Eastern Oregon University. (2020, October 30). "Psychology of Competitiveness." Retrieved July 25, 2023, from https://online.eou.edu/resources/article/psychology-of-competitiveness/.

Elliptic. (2019, September 18). "Bitcoin Money Laundering: How Criminals Use Crypto." Elliptic. Retrieved August 21, 2023, from https://www.elliptic.co/blog/bitcoin-money-laundering.

Farfan, M. (2023, February 8). "Retire Off BITCOIN by 2030 [How Much BTC??]." YouTube. Retrieved August 22, 2023, from https://www.youtube.com/watch?v=RCTIUZJQZ7I.

Federal Reserve. (2022, April 14). "2021 Federal Reserve Note Print Order Delivery." Board of Governors of the Federal Reserve System. Retrieved August 4, 2023, from https://www.federalreserve.gov/paymentsystems/files/currency_print_orders_2021d.pdf.

Federal Trade Commission. (2014, August 7). "How Consumers Win When Businesses Compete." Retrieved July 25, 2023, from https://www.ftc.gov/sites/default/files/attachments/competition-counts/zgen01.pdf.

Feign, A. (2022, September 19). "Blockchain Technology Explained: What Is a Blockchain and How Does it Work?" CoinDesk. Retrieved July 31, 2023, from https://www.coindesk.com/learn/what-is-blockchain-technology/.

Finbold. (2022, October 1). "Bitcoin to Surpass $12 Million by 2031 Fuelled by Collapsing Dollar, Says Ex-Hedge Fund Manager." Finbold. Retrieved August 22, 2023, from https://finbold.com/bitcoin-to-surpass-12-million-by-2031-fuelled-by-collapsing-dollar-says-ex-hedge-fund-manager/.

Foote, S. (2022, February 25). "El Salvador and the Potential for Low-Fee Crypto-Remittances. El Salvador and the Potential for Low-Fee Crypto-Remittances – Institute for Business in the Global Context." Retrieved August 17, 2023, from https://sites.tufts.edu/ibgc/el-salvador-and-the-potential-for-low-fee-crypto-remittances/.

Forrester Consulting. (2020, July). "The Total Economic Impact of Accepting Bitcoin Using BitPay." BitPay.com. Retrieved August 18, 2023, from https://bitpay.com/blog/content/files/2022/09/Forrester-TEI-Report-2021.pdf.

Frontier Bank. (2022, September 26). "Bitcoin vs. Traditional Finance - Part 2 — Frontier Bank: Bitcoin." Frontier Bank: Bitcoin. Retrieved August 17, 2023, from https://www.bitcoin.frontierbank.com/bitcoin-blog/bitcoin-vs-traditional-finance-part-2.

Ganne, E. (2018). "Can Blockchain Revolutionize International Trade?" World Trade Organization. Retrieved August 20, 2023, from https://www.wto.org/english/res_e/booksp_e/blockchainrev18_e.pdf.

Global Change Data Lab. (2023, June 13). "Electricity Production by Source." Our World in Data. Retrieved August 1, 2023, from https://ourworldindata.org/grapher/electricity-prod-source-stacked?facet=none&country=CHN~USA.

Global Radar. (2017, September 2). "The Potential Impact of Cryptocurrency on the Remittance Industry." Global RADAR. Retrieved August 18, 2023, from https://globalradar.com/the-potential-impact-of-cryptocurrency-on-the-remittance-industry/.

Go Globe. (2023, May 4). "Eye-Opening Statistics of Online Piracy in Numbers." GO-Globe. Retrieved August 20, 2023, from https://www.go-globe.com/online-piracy-in-numbers-facts-and-statistics-infographic/.

Goodman, L. M. (2014, March 6). "The Face Behind Bitcoin." *Newsweek*. Retrieved July 30, 2023, from https://www.newsweek.com/2014/03/14/face-behind-bitcoin-247957.html.

Greenspan, A. (2008, January 29). "Greenspan Admits the Federal Reserve Is Above the Law & Answers to No One." YouTube. Retrieved August 17, 2023, from https://www.youtube.com/watch?v=ol3mEe8TH7w.

Harvey, C. T. S. (2017, July 10). "Competition Is a Sin." HuffPost UK. Retrieved July 31, 2023, from https://www.huffingtonpost.co.uk/christopher-ts-harvey/competition-is-a-sin_b_17444620.html.

Hayek, F. A. (1976). "Denationalisation of Money: An Analysis of the Theory and Practice of Concurrent Currencies." Institute of Economic Affairs.

Hayek, F. A. (2023, March 19). "Why the Worst Get on Top." Mises Institute. Retrieved August 4, 2023, from https://mises.org/library/why-worst-get-top.

Hertig, A. (2021, February 8). "Which Crypto Projects Are Based on Ethereum?" Yahoo Finance. Retrieved August 2, 2023, from https://finance.yahoo.com/news/crypto-projects-based-ethereum-145710336.html.

IBM. (2022, September 26). "Blockchain for Supply Chain." IBM. Retrieved August 3, 2023, from https://www.ibm.com/blockchain-supply-chain.

Infinite Market Cap. (2023, August 4). "All Assets." Infinite Market Cap. Retrieved August 4, 2023, from https://8marketcap.com/.

Inflation Rates in the United States of America. (2023, August 4). Worlddata.info. Retrieved August 4, 2023, from https://www.worlddata.info/america/usa/inflation-rates.php.

Institutional Investor. (2014, July 23). "Understanding How Bitcoin Transcends Traditional Boundaries." Institutional Investor. Retrieved August 20, 2023, from https://www.institutionalinvestor.com/article/2bsum6b9lydpmw27uyg3k/portfolio/understanding-how-bitcoin-transcends-traditional-boundaries.

Jahani, J. (2021, October 9). "Crypto Remittances Are a Lifeline for the World's Most Vulnerable." TechCrunch. Retrieved August 18, 2023, from https://techcrunch.com/2021/10/09/crypto-remittances-are-a-lifeline-for-the-worlds-most-vulnerable/.

Jahosky, J. (2020, September 29). "Study Shows Merchants That Accept Bitcoin Attract New Customers and Sales." Business Wire. Retrieved August 18, 2023, from https://www.businesswire.com/news/home/20200929005406/en/Study-Shows-Merchants-That-Accept-Bitcoin-Attract-New-Customers-and-Sales.

Jefferson. (1776). "Transcript of Declaration of Independence (As Adopted)." Thomas Jefferson's Monticello. Retrieved August 17, 2023, from https://www.monticello.org/thomas-jefferson/jefferson-s-three-greatest-achievements/the-declaration/transcript-of-the-declaration/.

Jenkinson, G. (2023, May 11). "How the IRS Seized $10B Worth of Crypto Using Blockchain Analytics." Cointelegraph. Retrieved August 21, 2023, from https://cointelegraph.com/news/how-the-irs-seized-10b-worth-of-crypto-using-blockchain-analytics.

jgarzik. (2010, November 19). "Bitcoin Dev Log." Building Bitcoin. https://buildingbitcoin.org/bitcoin-dev/log-2010-11-19.html#l-1541.

Joël Valenzuela. (2016, April 26). "Bitcoin Transcends Borders, Creates Truly Global Economy." Cointelegraph. Retrieved August 18, 2023, from https://cointelegraph.com/news/bitcoin-transcends-borders-creates-truly-global-economy.

Joint Economic Committee. (2018, February 28). "The 2018 Joint Economic Report." Congress. Retrieved August 5, 2023, from https://www.jec.senate.gov/public/_cache/files/7faf912a-0fd2-4a92-bba4-e41c2c1f8e93/2018-joint-economic-committee-response.pdf.

Jones, A. (2021, May 23). "Bitcoin Oracle Says Maverick Cryptocurrency Going to All-Time Highs." The Alex Jones Show. Retrieved July 29, 2023, from https://www.banned.video/watch?id=60ab1f89ba189f450b9535c5.

Jones, D. (2023, May 10). "Bitcoin and Its Influence on International Trade." Market Business News. Retrieved August 18, 2023, from https://marketbusinessnews.com/bitcoin-and-its-influence-on-international-trade/332118/.

Kelion, L. (2017, July 20). "Bitcoin Swings as Civil War Looms." BBC. Retrieved July 30, 2023, from https://www.bbc.com/news/technology-40654194.

Kerr, E. (2022, May 12). "See How Much Inflation Is Costing You." US News Money. Retrieved July 25, 2023, from https://money.usnews.com/money/personal-finance/family-finance/articles/inflation-calculator-see-how-much-inflation-is-costing-you.

Keshner, A. (2021, August 17). "Western Union Suspends Money Transfers to Afghanistan, Cutting Off 'Vital Channel' of Financial Support." MarketWatch. Retrieved August 18, 2023, from https://www.marketwatch.com/story/how-to-help-people-in-afghanistan-as-western-union-suspends-money-transfers-into-the-country-11629225525.

kiba. (09, December 2010). "Bitcoin Developer Log." Building Bitcoin. https://buildingbitcoin.org/bitcoin-dev/log-2010-12-09.html#l-274.

Kilroy, A. (2023, July 15). "How Can I Tell If I'm Actually Rich?" Yahoo Finance. Retrieved July 25, 2023, from https://finance.yahoo.com/news/know-im-rich-140000452.html.

Krugman, P. (1998, June 10). "Why Most Economists' Predictions Are Wrong." Red Herring Online. Retrieved August 3, 2023, from https://web.archive.org/web/19980610100009/https://www.redherring.com/mag/issue55/economics.html.

Krugman, P. (2018, July 31). "Opinion | Transaction Costs and Tethers: Why I'm a Crypto Skeptic." (Published 2018) The New York Times. Retrieved August 3, 2023, from https://www.nytimes.com/2018/07/31/opinion/transaction-costs-and-tethers-why-im-a-crypto-skeptic.html.

La Monica, P. R. (2020, November 30). "Bitcoin Hits an All-Time High of Just Under $20,000." CNN. Retrieved July 29, 2023, from https://www.cnn.com/2020/11/30/investing/bitcoin-prices-record-high/index.html.

Lee, D. (2023, May 20). "Ledger Recover vs. Trezor (Software Engineer Explains)." YouTube. Retrieved August 15, 2023, from https://www.youtube.com/watch?v=Q7n9ue3GKx8.

Leech, O. (2022, October 31). "What Is the Bitcoin White Paper?" CoinDesk. Retrieved July 31, 2023, from https://www.coindesk.com/tech/2021/01/21/what-is-the-bitcoin-white-paper/.

Lennon, H., & Danise, A. (2021, January 19). "The False Narrative of Bitcoin's Role in Illicit Activity." Forbes. Retrieved August 21, 2023, from https://www.forbes.com/sites/haileylennon/2021/01/19/the-false-narrative-of-bitcoins-role-in-illicit-activity/.

Lima, C., & Schaffer, A. (2022, October 10). "Analysis | PayPal Faces Backlash after Floating Fines for Sharing Misinformation." Washington Post. Retrieved August 2, 2023, from https://www.washingtonpost.com/politics/2022/10/10/paypal-faces-backlash-after-floating-fines-sharing-misinformation/.

Loh, T. H. (2021, November 2). "An Analysis of Financial Institutions in Black-Majority Communities: Black Borrowers and Depositors Face Considerable Challenges in Accessing Banking Services." Brookings Institution. Retrieved August 2, 2023, from https://www.brookings.edu/articles/an-analysis-of-financial-institutions-in-black-majority-communities-black-borrowers-and-depositors-face-considerable-challenges-in-accessing-banking-services/.

Marte, J., & Nomiyama, C. (2021, April 15). "Black and Hispanic Firms Half as Likely to Get Needed Financing, Fed Study Finds." Reuters. Retrieved August 2, 2023, from https://www.reuters.com/business/finance/black-hispanic-firms-half-likely-get-needed-financing-fed-study-finds-2021-04-15/.

McCracken, T. (2022, March 29). "Top Non-Custodial Exchanges for Privacy and Security." The Coin Bureau. Retrieved August 14, 2023, from https://www.coinbureau.com/review/top-non-custodial-exchanges/.

MetaMaths. (2021, May 5). "Curves Which Make Bitcoin Possible." YouTube. Retrieved August 16, 2023, from https://www.youtube.com/watch?v=qCafMW4OG7s.

Mises Institute. (2014, November 28). "Denationalisation of Money: The Argument Refined." Mises Institute. Retrieved August 4, 2023, from https://mises.org/library/denationalisation-money-argument-refined.

Mpkomara. (2010, November 23). "Bitcoin Dev Log." Building Bitcoin. https://buildingbitcoin.org/bitcoin-dev/log-2010-11-23.html#l-1059.

Mubaslat, J. (2020, January 10). "What Is Money? And Could Bitcoin Be the Best One? | Jad Mubaslat | TEDxDayton." YouTube. Retrieved July 25, 2023, from https://www.youtube.com/watch?v=vROTmMzJnXk.

Murch. (2019, November 15). "Bitcoin." Stack Exchange. Retrieved August 10, 2023, from https://bitcoin.stackexchange.com/a/91719.

Mycryptopedia. (2022, April 24). "What Is SHA-256 and How Is It Related to Bitcoin?" Mycryptopedia. Retrieved August 8, 2023, from https://www.mycryptopedia.com/sha-256-related-bitcoin/.

Nakamoto, S. (2008, October 31). "A Peer-to-Peer Electronic Cash System." Bitcoin.org. Retrieved July 26, 2023, from https://bitcoin.org/bitcoin.pdf.

Nakamoto, S. (2009, February 11). "Bitcoin Open Source Implementation of P2P Currency." P2P Foundation. Retrieved July 26, 2023, from http://p2pfoundation.ning.com/forum/topics/bitcoin-open-source?id=2003008 percent3ATopic percent3A9402&page=1.

Nakamoto, S. (2010, August 27). "Re: Bitcoin Does NOT Violate Mises' Regression Theorem." Satoshi Nakamoto Institute. The Complete Satoshi. Retrieved August 2, 2023, from https://satoshi.nakamotoinstitute.org/posts/bitcointalk/428/.

Nakamoto Studies Institute. (2011, April 26). "Satoshi's Final Email to Gavin Andresen." Satoshi Nakamoto Email Index. Retrieved July 30, 2023, from https://nakamotostudies.org/emails/satoshis-final-email-to-gavin-andresen/.

Nayar, R. (2021, October 20). "How Bitcoin Brings Financial Literacy to Everyone." Bitcoin Magazine. Retrieved August 22, 2023, from https://bitcoinmagazine.com/culture/how-bitcoin-brings-financial-literacy.

99Bitcoins. (2017, September 21). "Bitcoin Transactions - from 'Send' to 'Receive.'" YouTube. Retrieved August 3, 2023, from https://www.youtube.com/watch?v=ZPFL6R-voW0.

99Bitcoins. (2018, July 12). "What Is Bitcoin Mining? (In Plain English)." YouTube. Retrieved August 17, 2023, from https://www.youtube.com/watch?v=BODyqM-V71E.

Novogratz, M. (2019, May 8). Mike Novogratz on Twitter: "I am shocked that @cz_binance even went there. Talk of forking or reorganizing the blockchain is close to heresy. When the ethereum community did it the project was like 5 months old. A baby. Bitcoin now has $100bn market cap." Twitter. Retrieved August 3, 2023, from https://twitter.com/novogratz/status/1126086058477858817.

OnlyOneTV. (2011, June 16). "The Bitcoin Show - Episode 003." YouTube. Retrieved July 30, 2023, from https://www.youtube.com/watch?v=MUfKOIU_K1I.

Paul, R. (1983). "The Founding Father's Premonition." The Reporter: The Student Newspaper at Miami Dade College. Retrieved August 21, 2023, from https://mdcthereporter.com/the-founding-fathers-premonition/.

Paul, R. (2019, November 18). "Federal Reserve: Enemy of Liberty and Prosperity." Ron Paul Institute for Peace and Prosperity. Retrieved July 26, 2023, from http://ronpaulinstitute.org/archives/featured-articles/2019/november/18/federal-reserve-enemy-of-liberty-and-prosperity/.

PK. (2023, April 01). "Historical US Home Prices: Monthly Median from 1953-2023. Don't Quit Your Day Job." Retrieved August 4, 2023, from https://dqydj.com/historical-home-prices/.

Polumbo, B. (2021, February 27). "What Is Bitcoin and What Makes It Special? An Economist Explains." Foundation for Economic Education. Retrieved August 21, 2023, from https://fee.org/articles/what-makes-bitcoin-special-an-economist-explains/.

Puri, S. (2023, July 4). "10 Years of Money Wisdom in Under 28 Minutes." YouTube. Retrieved July 25, 2023, from https://www.youtube.com/watch?v=5Q4Vth5CnPw.

PYMNTS. (2021, October 26). "New Study: Crypto Emerging as a Favored Form for Cross-Border Remittances." Pymnts.com. Retrieved August 18, 2023, from https://www.pymnts.com/cryptocurrency/2021/new-study-crypto-emerging-as-favored-form-for-cross-border-remittances/.

RAND Corporation. (2020). "Exploring the Use of Zcash Cryptocurrency for Illicit or Criminal Purposes." RAND Corporation. Retrieved August 21, 2023, from https://www.rand.org/content/dam/rand/pubs/research_reports/RR4400/RR4418/RAND_RR4418.pdf.

Redman, J. (2023, January 3). "14th Anniversary of Bitcoin's Genesis Block: A Look Back at the Birth of Cryptocurrency – Bitcoin News." Bitcoin.com News. Retrieved August 5, 2023, from https://news.bitcoin.com/14th-anniversary-of-bitcoins-genesis-block-a-look-back-at-the-birth-of-cryptocurrency/.

Ritchie, H., Mathieu, E., Roser, M., & Ortiz, E. (2023, August 3). "Internet. Our World in Data." Retrieved August 3, 2023, from https://ourworldindata.org/internet.

Rizzo, P. (2021, April 26). "10 Years Ago Today, Bitcoin Creator Satoshi Nakamoto Sent His Final Message." Forbes. Retrieved July 30, 2023, from https://www.forbes.com/sites/peterizzo/2021/04/26/10-years-ago-today-bitcoin-creator-satoshi-nakamoto-sent-his-final-message/?sh=5e6e082b10dd.

Rizzo, P. (2021, April 26). "What Happened When Bitcoin Creator Satoshi Nakamoto Disappeared." Bitcoin Magazine. Retrieved July 30, 2023, from https://bitcoinmagazine.com/technical/what-happened-when-bitcoin-creator-satoshi-nakamoto-disappeared.

Roosevelt, E. (Ed.). (1950). *F.D.R.: His Personal Letters, 1928-1945*. New York: Duell, Sloan and Pearce.

Roots, S. (2020, December 22). "Bitcoin Halving Dates and Price Charts: When Is the Next BTC Halving?" Changelly. Retrieved August 4, 2023, from https://changelly.com/blog/bitcoin-halving-2020-2024/.

Savvy Finance. (2023, July 19). "Michael Saylor - Just One Bitcoin Will Keep You Rich for Life." YouTube. Retrieved August 3, 2023, from https://www.youtube.com/watch?v-RKj-v6j6WrM.

Semega, J., & Kollar, M. (2022, September 13). "Income in the United States: 2021. U.S." Census Bureau. Retrieved July 25, 2023, from https://www.census.gov/library/publications/2022/demo/p60-276.html.

Seth, S. (2021, September 27). "Can Bitcoin Be Used for Overseas Remittances?" Investopedia. Retrieved August 18, 2023, from https://www.investopedia.com/tech/bitcoins-best-use-isnt-currency-its-overseas-remittances/.

ShadowOfHarbringer. (2010, November 02). "Bitcoin Is Not as Advertised." Bitcoin Forum. https://bitcointalk.org/index.php?topic=1647.msg19748#msg19748.

Sparks, H. (2021, May 24). "Infamous Bitcoin Pizza Guy Who Squandered $365M Haul Has No Regrets." New York Post. Retrieved August 4, 2023, from https://nypost.com/2021/05/24/bitcoin-pizza-guy-who-squandered-365m-has-no-regrets/.

Spike, J. (2021, September 17). "Hungary: Statue Honoring Mysterious Bitcoin Founder Unveiled." AP News. Retrieved July 29, 2023, from https://apnews.com/article/technology-business-arts-and-entertainment-hungary-blockchain-96a6b57589b73fd4e376fe5f91b022e3.

Spooner, L. (1870). "No Treason. No. VI. The Constitution of No Authority (1870)." Online Library of Liberty. Retrieved August 17, 2023, from https://oll.libertyfund.org/title/spooner-no-treason-no-vi-the-constitution-of-no-authority-1870.

Sristy, A. (2021, November 30). "Blockchain in the Food Supply Chain - What Does The Future Look Like?" Walmart Global Tech. Retrieved August 3, 2023, from https://tech.walmart.com/content/walmart-global-tech/en_us/news/articles/blockchain-in-the-food-supply-chain.html.

Stack Exchange. (2012, September 17). "Where and How Is Secp256k1 Used within Bitcoin?" Bitcoin Stack Exchange. Retrieved August 16, 2023, from https://bitcoin.stackexchange.com/questions/4732/where-and-how-is-secp256k1-used-within-bitcoin.

Statista. (2023, August 2). "Bitcoin Mining by Country 2022." Statista. Retrieved August 11, 2023, from https://www.statista.com/statistics/1200477/bitcoin-mining-by-country/.

Steele, C. (2018, May 21). "Bitcoin Transaction Explained in 5 Minutes." YouTube. Retrieved August 3, 2023, from https://www.youtube.com/watch?v=E4DOU0JdDRw.

Tětek, J. (2022, January 27). "What Is Nakamoto-Gresham's Law, And How Does It Pertain to Bitcoin?" Bitcoin Magazine. Retrieved August 22, 2023, from https://bitcoinmagazine.com/business/what-is-nakamoto-greshams-law.

Thompson, C. (2023, January 9). "The Five Words That Tell Me That Satoshi Nakamoto Is Dead." LinkedIn. Retrieved July 29, 2023, from https://www.linkedin.com/pulse/five-words-tell-me-satoshi-nakamoto-dead-clive-thompson/.

thrashaholic. (2010, 10 15). "Bitcoin Dev Log." Building Bitcoin. https://buildingbitcoin.org/bitcoin-dev/log-2010-10-15.html#l-201.

Thubron, R. (2021, August 4). "Study: More People Would Buy Crypto if They Found It Less Confusing." TechSpot. Retrieved August 14, 2023, from https://www.techspot.com/news/90662-study-more-people-would-buy-crypto-if-they.html.

Tikkanen, A., & Vaughan, D. (2020, January 31). "A Brief (and Fascinating) History of Money." Britannica. Retrieved July 26, 2023, from https://www.britannica.com/story/a-brief-and-fascinating-history-of-money.

Trezor. (2023, February 3). "Can I invest in Trezor?" Trezor. Retrieved August 15, 2023, from https://trezor.io/learn/a/for-investors.

Urban Caffeine. (2021, January 18). "Bitcoin White Paper Explained (Simplified and Visualized)." YouTube. Retrieved August 5, 2023, from https://www.youtube.com/watch?v=Dpqtav3oT4k.

Vermaak, W. (2023, July 1). "Bitcoin Whitepaper: Simplified for Everyone." CoinMarketCap. Retrieved August 1, 2023, from https://coinmarketcap.com/alexandria/article/bitcoin-whitepaper-simplified-for-everyone.

Visual Objects. (2020, April 8). "Nearly One-Third of People Believe Cryptocurrency Is Used Primarily for Illegal Purchases, but Actual Purchases May Be More Boring." PR Newswire. Retrieved August 3, 2023, from https://www.prnewswire.com/news-releases/nearly-one-third-of-people-believe-cryptocurrency-is-used-primarily-for-illegal-purchases-but-actual-purchases-may-be-more-boring-301037317.html.

Wallabit Media. (2017, September 4). "Bitcoin Price History Chart (2009, 2010 to 2023)." Buy Bitcoin Worldwide. Retrieved July 26, 2023, from https://buybitcoinworldwide.com/price/.

Ward, S. (2023, August 17). "Bitcoin Welcomes All, But It's No Haven for the Naive Criminal." Forbes. Retrieved August 21, 2023, from https://www.forbes.com/sites/digital-assets/2023/08/17/bitcoin-welcomes-all-but-its-no-haven-for-the-naive-criminal/?sh=20baf8303f0e.

Web3 Working Group. (2022, October 19). "What Is Public Key Cryptography?" YouTube. Retrieved August 1, 2023, from https://www.youtube.com/watch?v=SPeAZLfqm5k.

Wheelwright, T. (2018). "Tax-Free Wealth: How to Build Massive Wealth by Permanently Lowering Your Taxes." BZK Press, LLC.

Williams, C. (2021, January 3). "Bitcoin's Birthday: Satoshi Nakamoto's Hidden Message Explained." Crypto Briefing. Retrieved July 25, 2023, from https://cryptobriefing.com/bitcoin-birthday-satoshi-hidden-message-explained/.

Wilser, J., & Luo, X. (2022, December 20). "10 Predictions for the Future of Crypto in 2023." CoinDesk. Retrieved August 22, 2023, from https://www.coindesk.com/consensus-magazine/2022/12/20/10-predictions-for-the-future-of-crypto-in-2023/.

The World Bank. (2018, April 22). "Data | Identification for Development." ID4D. Retrieved August 15, 2023, from https://id4d.worldbank.org/global-dataset

Zahn, M. (2022, December 13). "A Timeline of Cryptocurrency Exchange: FTX's Historic Collapse." ABC News. Retrieved August 14, 2023, from https://abcnews.go.com/Business/timeline-cryptocurrency-exchange-ftxs-historic-collapse/story?id=93337035.

Printed in the USA
CPSIA information can be obtained
at www.ICGtesting.com
JSHW010402311023
51155JS00005B/14

9 798868 947353